You will know many, or at least, some, of these women - and I think you will love their faces and stories - you are always in my heart.
Meredith
august 2001

A Life Well-Rooted

WOMEN OF COLORADO'S ROARING FORK VALLEY

PHOTOGRAPHS
Meredith Ogilby

Narratives by the women, their families or friends

Hell Roaring Publishing
Carbondale, Colorado

Published 2001 in the United States of America
by Hell Roaring Publishing

Library of Congress Cataloging-in-Publication Data

Ogilby, Meredith W. 1944 -
A Life Well-Rooted: Women of Colorado's Roaring Fork Valley

ISBN 0-9709633-0-0

1. Women–West (U.S.) biography
2. West–photographs and narratives
3. Women–regional portraits–social life and customs

Printed by The Stinehour Press, Lunenburg, Vermont

A Life Well-Rooted

Table of Contents

Dedication

This book is for friends, daughters, husbands, grandparents, sisters, brothers, children and all who appreciate how story, anecdote, and an expression of values serve us in our efforts toward family, community, and the places we cherish. We know there are many more in our valley who would provide such inspiration and are sorry we either did not know who they were or simply had to finally have a last page.

Foreword

"I think what I admire most about my mother is her ability to enjoy and be comfortable with different lifestyles and people from all walks of life," says Darcey Brown. "And it's that same classless attitude that I admire most about the Roaring Fork Valley and hope can be preserved."

First you notice the faces: relaxed and often smiling, the eyes clear and direct. These women, whom photographer Meredith Ogilby meets in their favorite places, look like they really know how to laugh. Some, perhaps, could even tell a ribald joke.

But Elizabeth Arden, eat your heart out. It's not mascara on eyelids or blush on cheekbones that define the faces of the women of the Roaring Fork Valley of western Colorado. It's intelligence and frankness, plus a feisty edge: "I'm old enough to be proud of the fact that my Dad helped raise the flag on Iwo Jima," says Anita Witt. "I'm also young enough to wear tight jeans and fancy cowboy boots to town."

Some also reveal glee in recalling youthful pursuits: "I canned the loveliest cauliflower," says Beulah Wilson. Painter Bleu Stroud tells us she "developed a passion for mushroom hunting and one year I froze over 200 pounds of different varieties of mushrooms." A convert to winter camping in the 1950s as well, she spent nights under "a huge spruce tree with its lower branch tips tied onto the snow, forming a cozy tent all around. I shared it with a resident porcupine several times."

These women are no-nonsense types. They have chosen to live at more than mile-high altitudes: they know the mountains as both magnificent and perilous, and they've learned both how to adapt and how to cope. Some worry about increasing population pressure on their way of life. They are engaged. Mary Eshbaugh Hayes, a journalist and photographer of the area's denizens and celebrities for 50 years, startles us by staring piercingly at Ogilby's lens. Pat Fender shares a similarly direct gaze and disarms us by admitting, "At a very early age I knew I wanted to marry a rancher."

Nobody boasts, though some in this remarkable valley, home to Aspen and Glenwood Springs, have changed the world. Connie Harvey, Joy Caudill and Dottie Fox talk briefly about their work to preserve thousands of acres of wild lands for all Americans. Betty Pfister recalls that she was Colorado's first woman helicopter pilot, altering the "aerial landscape" of Aspen. Marlyn Fiscus, deadpan - allows that she retired "early" as a cook for the Colorado Rocky Mountain School. She was 84. Neva Daniel left college teaching at 70 to start a new career focusing on "intensive journal writing."

Eve Homeyer, the first woman mayor of Aspen and seemingly tough as the tree she leans on, still despises cars enough not to drive one. Look closely at the delightful portrait of Paula Mechau, 94, perched on the knee of her son, Mike. Knowing nothing about her you might guess that she is a woman of conviction and integrity - almost certainly a teacher who has worked hard all of her life. And you would be right.

But then, all of the women Ogilby introduces us to, share that attribute, whether the work is raising families or working for nonprofit groups, running ranches or pushing on government to protect public lands. Yet what's endearing about these women is that so many love to get their hands dirty. Like Laurie McBride, they can't wait for the snow to recede and the earth to grow warm so they can plant something gorgeous or good to eat - or both.They've come to know well the place they live in and what it can produce, provided you muck around in the ground. The women we meet here are almost certainly among those "stickers" writer Wallace Stegner heralded, those who stayed put to build a full life in the rural West. At the same time they helped build a vital community. Their achievement is something to cheer and to envy - particularly since they seem to be having an awfully good time!

by Betsy Marston

In 1975, Betsy Marston moved from New York to Paonia, Colorado, a town of 1,500 just over McClure Pass from the Roaring Fork Valley. She has been editor of "High Country News," which covers public land and rural community issues in the West, since 1983.

Index of Women

Introduction

This could be a book about you. If you have come to love a place – the place where your own story travels along beloved paths. If your soul awakens to the return of the bluebird, the arrival of a seed catalogue, sharp horizons and vast spaces. If, in the eyes or the hands of an older person, you sense story upon story that will reveal some truths that can be trusted. If you suspect that surprise builds character. If you yearn to return to the good earth some of what you have been given. If you like to hunt for your compass bearings in the life of another. If you know you must take care of a place or a person as change threatens to tear at its very essence. If a place is refuge. If you have said, "Aaah, I'm home."

Well-rooted to one woman means well-located, knowing how to get home when the time has come. To Meredith Ogilby, the photographer, whose portraits are within, a time has come to tie her extraordinary skills in portrait photography to stories of women whose identity comes from fastening a life to a place – putting down roots. Meredith traveled up and down the Roaring Fork Valley with bouquets, or eggs from her chickens, perhaps maple syrup from her birthplace in Wisconsin and always her camera, seeking to understand each woman before she chose the focus which you see within. The artist who could see in one face resolve, in another joy, in another hard-suffering patience brought forth the willingness from these women to extract from their lives stories which tell us something about the West and something about women and the beauty of adaptability.

In the portraits and in the narratives, the story of finding roots – in this case in rocky soil – during a century of change is full of adventure or hardship or monumental accomplishment or patience – but always a passion for this place – particularly the Roaring Fork Valley with a little extension into Wyoming. (One of the Hendricks girls pictured within just named her first-born Moxie Wyoming.) It is about how the generation before can share stories with the generation whose time is coming. It is about looking forward as we are grounded in the turn of seasons that help define us. "If I live until January," says Louiva Stapleton, "I know I have to live until spring. It is then I think about planting bulbs and get my garden catalogues."

It is our hope that in this mobile age, our readers will find the tenacity of roots.

by Adele Hause

Dorothea Farris and her daughter, Annie

"About a Sense of Place:
To me the landscape of the West reflects the character and the strength of the men and women who call this land home. Its stark beauty suggests openness and honesty; its sharp edges encourage directness; its forests offer solace; its clear skies demand clarity and vision; its mountains require risk. Evidence of past cultures and lifestyles mark the land. The piñons and cedars on the land I call home are scarred and bent from weather and time, but they survive and offer both strength and beauty as they reach ever for the sky. The overwhelming impression of this place is both of belonging and of freedom. One either feels one with the Earth or he must flee to the security of another place. This sense of place, this Life Well-Rooted, offers stability and permanence to our lives, and thus, allows us the freedom to do what we need to do and must do – care for, protect and preserve this special place.

About her daughter Annie:
She arrived smiling – laughing, actually – into this world. And, as the nurses tickled her toes in an attempt to make her yell and cry and clear her lungs, she gurgled and smiled and her eyes sparkled as she, fascinated, searched out the details of her new surroundings. We all knew then, as we know now, that the world is a better place because we share it with Annie. Her smiles and laughter light up the rooms she enters. She brightens the life of everyone she meets, and she watches, observes, and is fascinated by all she sees. The natural world belongs to Annie. She is among the few who enjoy a kinship with the wildness and the wildlife of the world. She is beauty and magic and joy and laughter. She is integrity and enthusiasm and warmth and love and sincerity. She is life at its finest. She is my daughter, my friend.

About freedom... and place:
From the time I was small I have a memory of a beautiful wall hanging in our house that served as a grounding philosophy for our upbringing. "There are only two lasting things we can leave our children – one is roots, the other is wings..." My parents did an incredible job of living by this philosophy – especially my mom. She has always been there for us, and she has always encouraged us to fly! I can't imagine two greater gifts one could give a person."

"To me the landscape of the West reflects the character and the strength of the men and women who call this land home. Its stark beauty suggests openness and honesty; its sharp edges encourage directness; its forests offer solace; its clear skies demand clarity and vision; its mountains require risk."

Paula Mechau and son, Mike

"Teachings on a Stairway

My grandmother is up at the old house now, touching all the old things, making sure all is well with the world. This morning she is standing at the kitchen window facing east and doing her leg exercises, head erect and well back, like a ballerina at the barre. She is ninety-four and still inclined to dance a little jig when she tells her age – a habit which took hold, I think, when she was in her early seventies.

Dante writes about coming into a dark and terrible wood in the middle of his life. Well, so did I, and when I did, I sought refuge with my two children in the house of my grandmother, at the headwaters of our family. It seems to me, now, that all of the really important conversations we had took place in my favorite part of the house, the stairway. There is a warm red color to the wooden banisters which would give anyone pause. At night we would ascend together, the children already sleeping above. Imagine two climbers, seeking footholds, hands on the shining banister, feet on the dusty trail. We proceeded slowly and without stopping.

It was on those stairs, after I had had a particularly dismal long distance call, that she turned around. She took my shoulders, looking with some intensity into my face – something she couldn't have done anywhere else – and said, "Hold the right thought. Everything will work out for the best if you will just hold the right thought." She had said this to me, to others, many times, countless times, as I was growing up. I had never heard it. It is the young, really, who are deaf.

If you had looked in on us precisely two weeks later, at the same hour, you would have found us starting up the stairs. I was feeling more deflated than, even now, I would want to admit. She had just trounced me at Scrabble. As we had cleared away the board and had tea, I had observed her avidity for the game cool to a species of noblesse oblige. She is excessively kind after a good win. So there we were going up shortly before midnight, and again she turned around on the stair. "You know," she said, "it is so important to keep in touch with inspirational material. What are you reading? Something uplifting, I hope." This last was delivered in a doubtful tone. How many times had I heard these words? We went off to our beds, full of our own thoughts. I had heard what I needed to hear. This is what I had come for."

by her granddaughter, Mally Mechau Strong

"She is ninety-four and still inclined to dance a little jig when she tells her age – a habit which took hold, I think, when she was in her early seventies."

Paula Mechau

"Paula Mechau meets me at the door of her home in Redstone. She is 92, full of grace, beautiful. I warn her that this time we are going to talk about her, not her husband, Frank. Frank died in 1946. "I feel my life with Frank was very important," she counters. "Not only was he an artist, but he was an extraordinary father and husband. Once I got married to Frank, I was in support of what he was doing. I wanted to be helpful in any way I could be." We sit in the kitchen and when we stand for a stretch, we see out the window one doe, then another, carefully venture from the Aspen grove toward the house. "Oh, I love it here," Paula says.

Her loves: Frank, her home, her children, the Crystal River Valley. Before the Crystal River Valley there was New York, marriage, a one-way passage to Paris for $700 in 1929 so Frank could study art, a job offered to Paula so they could remain there, the birth of their first child, Vanni, a return to the United States in the midst of the depression, 1932. By the time they returned, Frank had received a nice write-up at an exhibition of American artists indicating he would be a great mural artist. Paula almost forgets that it was necessary she get a job taking the census even though Frank had various opportunities to teach. "It was wonderful that Roosevelt introduced the opportunity to compete for murals," Paula remembers.

The young couple moved to the West and lived in Denver where son Dorik was born and later in Colorado Springs where Frank was offered a job at the Broadmoor Art Academy, now the Colorado Springs Fine Art Center. Home to Frank had been Glenwood Springs and it was from Glenwood that one day in the late thirties they traveled up to Redstone. All of the buildings were empty, the lavish days of Colorado Fuel and Iron glory having vanished. "Let's go look at the clocktower," Frank said to Paula speaking of the Redstone Inn. "All of a sudden a black man in a white jacket came out!" Paula brings the moment up close. "Mrs. Macdonald, the third wife of JC Osgood, saw us there, welcomed us, and asked where we were from. As we visited she told us that for the first time she was selling houses individually and wondered if we were interested. Frank leaned over and whispered to me, 'Do you realize nobody lives here?' I didn't care, it was so beautiful and I answered 'What is the price?'"

The price was $1800 and that house was traded in 1945 for her current home – now the shrine to Paula's loves. Though the talented artist, Frank Mechau, died in 1946, he lives in that home today in his paintings and the large dining room he crafted, and he seems still to be Paula's companion. Through these years 1939 to 1946, the family learned how to survive in the mountains. At one time, they all returned to New York because Frank was offered the job of heading the Department of Painting and Sculpture at Columbia University, but in one year it seemed best for Paula and the children to return to Redstone. "The children craved returning and knew they would have work to do if we were to live in Redstone," she explains. Frank soon returned as well. "We couldn't have gotten along without trout and deer," Paula says, and she recalls as well the fact that electricity was only turned on when

Mrs. Macdonald came to Redstone. Vanni tied flies and sold them to fishermen. They had a garden. They bought 100 Rhode Island reds. The children helped with many of the chores.

There is poetry in Paula's voice. No wonder. She shared her love for great literary masters with her family. "I would read aloud to them in the evening and then have a discussion. We were fairly isolated and we had a strong family as a result," she reflects. She has continued reading aloud her favorite authors to her children and to students until recently. She often read to Frank as he worked. She also taught the children ballads by plunking a note on the piano to get a key and then line by line teaching them the song. "We sang together when we had company. Once we were invited to sing in Aspen at the same time Burl Ives was giving a concert. A man approached us after the concert and said 'I work with the Metropolitan Opera and I think I could find a way for you to be included in a series of concerts.' Paula responded that it would have to be after school time and the family became traveling folksingers.

"I was like a mother duck as we went on tour performing here and there. The children would follow me in and we would begin singing. We were never very self-conscious. Dorik drove for most of our tours. The newspaper responses were marvelous." When they were in Redstone, they would be invited to sing at the Mansion or the Lodge, now known as the Redstone Castle. Paula taught folk-singing for years after her children were grown in the public schools and at Colorado Rocky Mountain School where she also taught weaving and served as secretary to John Holden.

Many students at Colorado Rocky Mountain School recall experiences with Paula. Included is a story which provides a glimpse into her character by a former student from the fifties when students were confined to a smoking porch for that particular vice.

"I never even questioned Paula's motives for coming to the smoking porch, but that's where I first got to know her. She was definitely unorthodox in choosing to join the students out there, and it was part of Paula's unorthodox character that made her presence so welcome. What school-age people need more than anything else from the adult world is 'respect,' to be treated by adults as if the young person's emotions and ideas were worth some genuine attention! It was certainly the central factor in my early friendship with Paula, who came out onto that smoking porch looking to do intellectual battle with anyone she found, her wits sharpened, her tongue courteous but unrestrained.

"Those who have known Paula over the years are probably used to thinking of her as one of the intellectual guiding spirits of the school and as one of its unflinching moral invigilators. Fewer of us, perhaps think often of her greatest gift to us, her deep and abiding care for the school and for the countless individuals in the school community who have been blessed to know her."

CRMS Alumnus, Alan "Mac" Watson

by Adele Hause

"I was like a mother duck as we went on tour performing here and there. The children would follow me in and we would begin singing."

Pat Fender

"At a very early age I knew I wanted to marry a rancher. It's extremely fortunate that Bill Fender was willing to share a ranch life with me and that I was also able to be involved in the educational and creative efforts of the faculty at the Colorado Rocky Mountain School even if only on a peripheral basis. Married life began in July, 1954, and my assorted jobs at CRMS began in September of the same year. I know I sometimes neglected my family because of my job and I regret having worked at all when our children were very little, but I have loved the combination of these two different worlds. Our friends in agriculture and at the school have been so varied and interesting.

Our first home was right where Emma and David Danciger live now on Prince Creek, but it was a small log cabin. What a fabulous view – Mt. Sopris to the south, Carbondale and Red Hill to the northwest. Bill added a bathroom to the house a week before our wedding. In 1957 we began renting the ranch ground at the school and Bill managed that for four years.

When we moved to our ranch in Emma in 1960, all the homes on the south side of the Roaring Fork river were farmhouses. Can you imagine that in the 1960s we moved our cows and calves from Emma down Highway 82 to graze our rented pasture (now the Ranch at Roaring Fork) for several weeks? Then we trailed them over the Carbondale bridge to Lewie Thompson's fields (now the River Valley Ranch) to rest overnight. Early the next morning, we'd leave for the Redstone pasture hoping not to meet too many fast coal trucks on Highway 133.

What a sorrow now to drive from Basalt to Glenwood Springs and see how rapidly the rural beauty is disappearing from the valley floors. It's hard to explain why ranching is such a compelling way of life to me and why it is so wrenching to know it is vanishing. To see a new calf running in the sunshine or fields that are green because they were irrigated by your husband or son is a great pleasure. So is the sight of our daughter out in a snowstorm helping her brother. Visions of a life-style rooted in nature."

"What a sorrow now to drive from Basalt to Glenwood Springs and see how rapidly the rural beauty is disappearing from the valley floors."

Emmy Neil and her granddaughter, Lindsey

"Emmy began teaching in a four-room schoolhouse in Burns, Colorado. After the children were moved to a larger school, the yard was full of sagebrush. There was to be a track day at Gypsum and all schools were invited. "I had a Ford convertible with a rumble seat they loved to ride on. We cleared out the stumps and sage as much as we could – went around the schoolyard and measured – practiced running in recesses and lunch, and then hacked out more sagebrush. I said to the students beforehand that the boys and girls would be wearing shorts and tennis shoes at the track meet. None of these kids had ever worn a pair of shorts in their lives. The boys wore overalls and work boots and the girls wore dresses. We were the laughing stock and we took almost every blue ribbon. Then it came down to the pole vaulting. A small boy from Redcliff and our student, Verne kept competing. Finally the Redcliff boy won. Here was the kid with tennis shoes and here was Verne, clump, clump, clump!"

Emmy taught 4H sewing in Glenwood for 30 years. When Colorado Mountain College opened in the mid-sixties she became the first teacher in 'offspring' towns. The county agent knew how she had taught sewing for years and thought she was ideal for traveling to all of the small towns to teach. She teaches sewing, tailoring, knitting, quilting and cross-stitching in Rifle, Carbondale, Aspen, and Glenwood. "It's kind of like the one-room schoolhouse."

Since 1991 Emmy has taken her skills to Teotecacinte, Nicaragua as a result of Professor Dave Harmon's efforts through Colorado Mountain College to start a sister city project with Glenwood Springs. "Someone needs to be there to get the women together because they are so busy. Some of them still have a lot of children." She adds that some are paying attention to birth control. She took her granddaughter, Lindsey, with her soon after. Lindsey felt badly that the kids couldn't go to school after sixth grade and asked "What would it take to have a high school in Teotecacinte?" About a million pennies was the answer. "So she came home, got jars, and set them on teachers' desks throughout the valley and collected $11,000. Not all in pennies." They built a high school. They feel the project is now strong enough to be on its own."

by Adele Hause

"What would it take to have a high school in Teotecacinte? About a million pennies was the answer."

Neva Daniel

"I came to the Roaring Fork Valley in the mid-sixties. I was the first teacher hired by Colorado Mountain College. I was attracted to this new college that had innovative ideas. Having come from pioneering people, I liked the challenge of exploration.

I taught literature at CMC until I was seventy. Then I started a new career of facilitating the Progoff method of Intensive Journal writing and continued until I was eighty-five. This I took on the road. Besides giving workshops up and down the valley, I presented workshops in the western states and in Canada. My graduate studies and teaching all had to do with the symbolic process. I was fascinated by the power of words: words that heal, words that harm, and ultimately words that lead to self-discovery.

My greatest treasure is my family: my daughter Sharon, my daughter and son-in-law, Judy and Mike Wadyko, and my son and daughter-in-law, David and Audrey Daniel, my five grandchildren, nine great grandchildren, and one great, great grandchild.

"The Song of the Quick-Running Squash Plant"
By Neva Daniel

I wanted to be a quick-running squash plant
Growing exuberantly six inches a day
Glorious green energy surging, surging through
  my veins
Pulsing my vines capriciously up into a tree at the
  garden's edge
Huge golden-throated blossoms
Trumpeting, trumpeting
Then the emerging fruits
Enormous pale green bellies
Filled with seeds and immortality!
Absurdly hanging from the tree branch
Ah what fruition!"

by Neva Daniel

"I remember visiting Neva at Heritage Park Care Center a few years ago. I walked in terribly worried that "this might be it." She was in her room, and I knew immediately that she was going to make it. With her wonderful chuckle, she said she was concerned about the people in this place, that none of them seemed to know who the President was or what day it was, that everyone was asking, and did I know? I said I wasn't sure about the day but I thought I could come up with the President. She hushed me and told me to be careful not to let the nurses hear because they'd put me in the room next to the nursing station if I could not get the day right. It was so typical Neva, finding humor not insult in the patronizing attitude of the nursing staff. Although she was very sick, Neva had already formed a close friendship with one of the nurses, and she insisted upon spending most of her day at the front desk where "all the action is," that she wasn't going to be making doilies or paste cakes, and by the way, the tapes of Dante's *Inferno* were fascinating, had I read it? Neva was always on to something new. Every decade she would start a new program or study group, and every decade there would be twenty or thirty new "students" captivated by her wisdom and compassion. Her home was like a salon with visitors of all ages and interests; time with her was always a spiritual and intellectual experience."

by Darcey Brown

"Neva was always on to something new."

Patsy Forbes with daughter Janice and granddaughter Kate

"I am Patsy's son, Janice's husband and Kate's father. I grew up in Aspen as the oldest son in a family of five, an older brother to three wonderful sisters. As the only boy in a family of women, I was revered, as we all noted, for no particular reason. I was immune to chores, and I was doted upon, even though, as my grandmother pointed out, "men were not all they are cracked up to be." It all began with my grandmother. My grandmother, my mother's mother, was adored by all, even my father during their divorce. When I was a child, I worried that my grandmother would die before me, and I knew that I couldn't bear it.

My life has always been anchored to solid ground by powerful women: my grandmother, my mother, my wife and my daughter. My mother gave me relentless love and a sense of who I am. Janice has impeccable integrity and has inspired me to always be a better person, to be more than I was cracked up to be. I can not imagine loving anyone more than her. Kate is the chief, she has her father's number, but calls it only when he (me) needs some humorous and loving reflection to help him see where not to go. She is the latest, the youngest and perhaps the wisest of all.

The collective wisdom, passion, grace and generosity sitting on those steps has always given me great comfort and relentlessly reminds me of the infinite possibility available in our world.

by AO Forbes

Here I am – one lucky lady with one of my eleven grandchildren, Kate, and my dear daughter-in-law, Janice. It took me a long time to get to such a blissful state – three husbands, the Marine Corps (my biggest mistake) and years of teaching in my own pre-school in Aspen, Casey Jr. High in Boulder, and a nursery school of mine in Santa Barbara. At 72, I met my final and best gentleman, Louis Tanenbaum. I hit the jackpot and am now enjoying 75 years with a modicum of aches and pains."

by Patsy Sweetser Forbes

"The collective wisdom passion, grace and generosity sitting on those steps has always given me great comfort and relentlessly reminds me of the infinite possibility available in our world."

Sis

Martha Downer Waterman with sister Mary Downer Evans

"Encouraged by their children and grandchildren, Martha Downer Waterman and Mary Downer Evans sat down to multiple sessions of recollection and dialogue to record their upbringing in the Roaring Fork Valley. In the fall of 2000 they published *Sis: The Tale of Two 'Sis'ters* depicting their family history beginning in Basalt in the early 1900s and in Aspen in the 1920s and '30s.

Mary recalls, "When we got to Basalt, it was the year of the 1918 flu epidemic and Daddy wouldn't allow Sis to go to school. In fact we weren't allowed out of the yard. In Basalt there was no doctor so Daddy helped take care of the sick."

Martha began her twenty-six-year career in 1933 at the Old Snowmass one-room schoolhouse. She also taught at the Rock Creek School where the BRB cabins up the Crystal River are now. In 1937, while she was teaching in Sterling, Colorado she and Leroy Waterman married. Leroy began building the Castle Creek Cabins in Aspen at that time which eventually included eight cabins and a service station. In 1953 they added onto the service station, providing space for a small grocery and called it Waterman's. In 1958 they decided to retire and they traded the block they owned in Aspen for a ranch in Basalt. "We got unretired in a hurry," Martha claimed, recalling that at the time they knew very little about ranching. Over the years on the ranch, Martha and Leroy took on many endeavors. They remodeled the house under the tutelage of a former Frank Lloyd Wright student, raised American Saddlebred horses to show, and later, after they sold the horses, raised registered cattle.

Of the horses she said, "At one time we had twelve colts. We always tried to have a mare's foal at the first of the year so the horse would be the age of the year. Of course that also happens to be the coldest time of the year, so we'd take a sleeping bag out to the barn to be sure we'd be there when the mare was going to foal. Sometimes you would anticipate it for a week."

In 1978 Martha retired from teaching. Soon after, she and her daughter traveled to Germany and it was there that she was inspired to turn her home into a bed and breakfast. Enjoying the company of her guests, she still runs the B&B today. "I celebrated my eighty-eighth birthday in March. I figure I won't do the bed and breakfast more than another twelve years, that'd make me one hundred and I think that'll be old enough.""

by Molly Ogilby

"I figure I won't do the bed and breakfast more than another twelve years, that'd make me one hundred and I think that'll be old enough."

Alice Rachel Sardy

"When Alice Rachel and her husband Tom first moved to Aspen in 1938 there were 707 residents. "Mostly old people were living in Aspen at the time. There wasn't anything for the young ones to do, so they would leave," Alice Rachel reports. "That spring of course I was busy, but I was a little unhappy. Then the summer was nice, and the fall was one of our beautiful, beautiful falls. And by then I had adjusted, and I've never changed my mind."

I sat with Alice Rachel on the porch of the Sardy house on Main Street in Aspen, her home for forty years before it became a guest-house and restaurant. We looked out together at what is now a non-stop busy street, and at Sayre Park and Ajax Mountain. "I planted nasturtiums along the wrought-iron fence and they did so well there, it seemed to be a suitable place for them. I had peonies in the corner, and there were two great big spruce trees." The nasturtiums, same as she used to plant, still sentinels along the fence, are vibrant even in the evening shadow. I pressed her with more questions of her early years with Tom in Aspen, desirous to reproduce the past.

"We moved to Aspen in 1938 from Monte Vista, Colorado, my husband Tom and I. We moved because we bought the business, Aspen Hardware and Supply. My husband and I had just been married for a year and a half. We were looking for a business and there weren't many on the market, but this one was. So we decided we'd come over and give it a try. We thought maybe we'd make it five years. And then Aspen started growing, skiing was just starting to get popular, more people were coming and we liked it so we just stayed."

For the first seven years Alice Rachel and Tom lived in an apartment above the Aspen Hardware and Supply. They started the first mortuary in Aspen as well. They bought what was later called the Sardy house, originally owned by the Atkinsons and built in 1892. The handsome brick house is where they remained for forty years. They moved the mortuary to the ground floor and were just a few blocks from the hardware store. As we sat on the porch Alice Rachel remembered that Sayre Park across the street used to be a dump until her husband initiated a clean up and the declaration of a town park. The library was next door for many years. What is now the Main St. Bakery and Cafe used to be a home.

Alice Rachel raised two children in Aspen, Sylvia and TJ. "The town was small enough so that you always knew where your children were - it was a wonderful place to raise them." Alongside her role as mother and wife, Alice Rachel volunteered much of her time and energy. She had a list of her activities when I first met with her, demonstrating her commitment to the town and her active role in society. "I loved living in Aspen and I loved the volunteer work I did." Her list included volunteer work at the hospital as a blue lady, helping at the Aspen Historical Society, the Aspen Chapel, the PTA and the House and Gardens Tour."

by Molly Ogilby

"I planted nasturtiums along the wrought-iron fence and they did so well there, it seemed to be a suitable place for them."

Kit Strang

"Well rooted" I probably am. An old cowboy would say I was 'located,' like the cow who knew how to get there, find the water, feed and get home when the time came...an important ingredient in managing the herd.

In addition to those fundamental ingredients, my roots are secured by a strong family. After thirty-nine years of ranching, thirty-four on this home place, with my husband, Michael, and our four children, Lathrop, Scott, Laurie and Bridget, the roots grow deep. Two children choose to live on this piece of land, and the other two visit with their spouses and children whenever possible. Beloved families of dogs, horses and a few special cats are also an important part of that root system. Descendants of the same old cow still raise their calves in the pastures. The meadows grow hay for the animals and turf to sell. They are beautiful, ever changing and always the same, as is the stately mountain called Sopris.

This bit of farmland has also been deeply enriched by the many people who have spent time here. They have come from everywhere - British Isles, Europe, Scandinavia, New Zealand, Australia, and many parts of these United States. There have been horsemen, cattlemen, politicians, riders, skiers, climbers, relatives, strangers, old school friends, as well as our children's friends. Some have stayed and many come back again and again to claim and cultivate their bit of Western Colorado. All continue to broaden and enrich our lives.

We have indeed been fortunate to have landed on such fertile soil where roots grow deep and wide.

"Beloved families of dogs, horses, and a few special cats are an important part of that root system."

Margaret Dunand Cerise, son Reno and grandson Johnny

"Delicately I walked through the past with Margaret. And understandably she was reluctant to go there. In 1929, at the age of sixteen, Margaret immigrated to Basalt from northern Italy with her mother and older brother to reunite with their father. Her father had worked in the gold mines in Italy and didn't want his son to do the same. With difficulty, Margaret explained to me that shortly after their arrival, her father and brother passed away, mysteriously poisoned, leaving her and her mother alone. In 1934 Margaret married, and she and her husband, Mela, bought his mother's ranch near Basalt.

I asked her what her life was like on the ranch and if she worked right alongside her husband. "Oh yes!" she replied. "When I got married I didn't know how to milk the cows, so I had to learn." Life was a continuum of action with all the chores and three children. All the clothes were washed by hand and there were times when the well went dry and water had to be hauled all the way from the river. She had a big garden where she grew all her vegetables that she canned each year for the winter. They had fresh milk and she made cheese for her family and also to sell. In addition to the cattle, they also raised chickens and pigs. While we sat in the living-room of her blue house in Basalt, she remembered a story of her pigs and of the ranch.

"It was when she didn't show up for a couple of meals that I figured the mother pig ran off, so I had to go look for her. When I found her she had died and there were six little pigs running around her. I brought them back and raised them on corn meal and milk. I dug out a piece of rotten wood to make a trough and dug out under the shop so that they could have a safe place to live. They used to follow me around and pull at my socks. They must have thought that I was their mother. Yes, all six survived." "

by Molly Ogilby

"When I got married I didn't know how to milk the cows, so I had to learn."

Eve Homeyer

"Eve moved to Aspen after the death of her husband, Harry, in June of 1959. After becoming active in politics, Eve was elected Aspen's first female mayor; she served three years. Of her experience she told me: "I didn't have any role models...what I did was what I thought ought to be done. That's how I saw it...I was a practical mayor, I felt like I was sort of a super housekeeper, cleaning this place up." Vigorously true to her word, Eve established standards and implemented public works which are still in evidence today. Eve set principles for herself as well, principles she not only preached but practiced.

Since 1970 to this day, Eve has not owned a car. She either walks, rides with friends or uses public transportation. "I have managed and it's become my thing. The first days of no cars in town happened my last year... You can see how well that went over. Instead, we closed off just a couple of blocks to see what it would be like. So I was in on the beginning of the malls. Some people have been just furious with me. They thought I would ruin their business. But the property that's on the mall now gets five times the rent it used to get."

When Eve was running for office, she remembered a General Motors engineer who said there would be electric cars within the year. "So I said I would never drive another polluting car, because I was going to buy an electric car. I called him up and told him I'd won and he didn't sound so happy. And I said to send me an electric car. He said they had some brochures. Anyhow, I thought I'd keep my word while I was mayor and I did. I had a big Oldsmobile and a Jeep and I sold them both." That was 1970. At eighty-four years old Eve keeps her word and still does not drive a car.

Curious about what makes a woman so courageous, determined and active, I asked Eve what she liked about herself. I wanted to know what strengths she thought she brought to her work and life. After chuckling at my, perhaps, intrusive question, she answered: "Good humor, good health... I suppose my ability to pace myself is good. He (my husband) taught me that money is not the end-all, it is the way to do what you want to do, and when you have enough, you have enough. Don't just stack it up. I think that's a valuable lesson, because I've never been one to say I've got to make more money, got to make more money. I'm glad I know how to work. I'm glad I'm willing to work – to keep busy. I think that work is terribly important. You have to know when enough is enough; you have to divide your life up so you don't spend all your time grubbing or all your time loafing. I guess that would be the basis of my philosophy – to enjoy it along the way.""

by Molly Ogilby

"I was a practical mayor. I was like a sort of super housekeeper cleaning this place up."

Mary Lamprecht Ferguson

"Carbondale lost Mary Ferguson in March of 1999. She lived first in Spring Gulch and then in Carbondale for all of her 92 years and was mother, wife, teacher, town councilwoman, and a DJ for public radio with her show "This I Remember."

Mary was a teacher for thirty-seven years. Her career began in a one-room schoolhouse and ended with thirteen years at the Carbondale Elementary School. She served on the Carbondale Town Board from 1984 to 1994. She was beloved, honored, and respected by all.

Upon receiving the "Career Woman of the Year" award from the Glenwood Business and Professional Women's Club and later Zeta Epsilon's "Carbondale Woman of the Year" award she said, "Even as a small child, I wanted to be a teacher. There was so much to know, and I knew so little...so I was always searching for something. Perhaps that is why it is such a thrill now to hear some little child exclaim, 'Say, teacher, did you know this?' and to hear for the first time some fact or truth which lights up the little child's mind. Children are great. The greatest! In one fell swoop, they can build you up or mow you down. Never underestimate them."

Mary volunteered numerous hours at the Near New Store for the Rebekahs, where she was a member since 1924, and for organizations including the Retired Senior Volunteer Program, the Mt. Sopris Historical Society, the Carbondale Public Education Foundation and KDNK.

Mary worked tirelessly to organize the Mt. Sopris Historical Society Museum, which is housed in the old Thompson family homesteader's cabin on highway 133 in Carbondale. Her passion was driven by the need for "the community to remember where we came from," said Lew Ron Thompson at Mary's memorial service.

It is no wonder that her passing marked the end of an era, but is just as important that it guides the beginning of a new one. She accepted change and worked with great cheer to bring the new and old together, considering the human sense of issues. "She was often a very effective conscience for the community," said former mayor, Bill Gray. "She reminded us of the saying that 'those who don't know their history are doomed to repeat it'." "

by Adele Hause

"It is such a thrill to hear some little child exclaim 'Say teacher, did you know this?' and to hear for the first time some fact or truth which lights up the little child's mind."

Anita Witt

"I'm old enough to be proud of the fact that my Dad helped raise the flag on Iwo Jima. I'm also young enough to wear tight jeans and fancy cowboy boots to town!

When Snowfoot, my horse, was born he rolled away from the mare, and I walked down to look at him. He looked up at me and let out the tiniest little whinny. To this day, he thinks I'm his mother because he saw me first.

My women friends are all cowgirls, even the ones who don't ride horses. They have grit and enough 'where-with-all' to take in stride the bad bumps life gives them.

There was a time when I wore slinky, sequined gowns and fancy high heels, but even then, I missed my jeans and boots.

Riding my horse Whiskey in the Rockies is just about the best – Of course, ropin' and singin' aren't bad either.

I knew a lady named Beulah Wilson who was almost a hundred years old when she died. She couldn't see, couldn't walk, couldn't even begin to take care of herself. Yet, she just lay there on her bed with such dignity, spoke so eloquently, and never once forgot her manners.

Walking with my dog Sadie around the ranch is one of the most peaceful times on earth. To see the deer and elk and the snow on Mt. Sopris is a gift that most people in the world will never be given.

I read about a cowgirl who used the expression "Always saddle your own horse." It has a lot more to do with life than horses, and sometimes it takes us a while to learn that."

"I read about a cowgirl who used the expression 'Always saddle your own horse.' It has a lot more to do with life than horses, and sometimes it takes us a while to learn that."

Pat Kearns Maddelone and Luetta Kearns Whitson

"My last visit with sisters Pat Maddalone and Luetta Whitson began at the Snowmass rodeo grounds and Wild Horse Ranch at Brush Creek, property that at one time was owned and operated by their parents. We spent the remainder of our afternoon at the now renovated Little Red Schoolhouse. Both women had attended the one room school through eighth grade. Pat remembers, "We left in the dark and got home in the dark. I remember it being cold all winter long, every year. We rode the horse to school and felt the cold metal of the stirrups. They didn't have those insulated boots like they do now, only the rubber overshoes. By the time you got to school your feet would be cold and never warm up! I read in the *New York Times* not long ago a study in the Northeast about people who grew up in this kind of environment, only went to one school, had one teacher, and how individual they became, how self-motivated. It's really true. You'd be sitting in the back of the room, in the second grade but somebody in the front in the seventh grade was learning something about geography that you might be interested in, and you could listen in. You were listening in."

"Grandmother Crosby walked over Independence Pass from Leadville around 1880. As I recall, she started out in a stagecoach. Some of the people got out and she was one of the people who got out and walked."

I asked the sisters about life in Aspen in the 40s during the war years. "When we were in school during the war, they turned school out for kids to go pick potatoes. We picked every day, long days, Sunday too. Hardest work I ever did in my life. It really hurts your back."

They both recall Aspen life in the forties: "The 10th Mountain Division, they were all over town in their white coats, ski parkas and skis. The Jerome Hotel had what was called a buffet. There was a bar there and a soda fountain - they had booths and a kind of dance floor. We'd go in there when we were in high school, we'd get a milk shake and the 10th Mountain would be in there, the night crew, and they'd be having Kruds. Boilermakers and Kruds. The Midnight Mine crew would be coming down, with their mining helmets on, and they'd have a shot and a beer, and everyone was visiting and music was playing. We went there every day! It would be a kind of scandal today, if they found a kid in there now, wouldn't it?"

Both bad weather and the end of late afternoon light were moving in as we talked and drank tea at a picnic table outside the Little Red Schoolhouse, so Pat ended with some final thoughts on Aspen. "Aspen allows you to be as eccentric as you want. I think you can move easily from one group to another. That aspect seems natural and right to us. I think it's even more obvious when you look at your children and grandchildren. They move like a stream of water - it's so seamless in the way people move among people. I think that's more of a western attitude than in other places, because you were so dependent on each other and because of your isolation. That was true growing up on the ranch. You'd have somebody who was a sheepherder from the next ranch sitting at the dinner table, you'd have somebody come by to sell a warm blanket, and the hired men might have been from any place, and there was no difference.""

by Meredith Ogilby

"They move like a stream of water – it's so seamless in the way people move among people."

Adele Hause and grandsons, Weaver and Eric Froelicher

"My roots are tangled and I like it that way. When I came with my first husband to the Colorado Rocky Mountain School in 1961, a magic overtook me – of the school, the land and the community. In fact, the school has probably opened my eyes more to the beauty we fortunate ones have settled in than anything else has – even the dominant and lovely features of the landscape. That is because of the CRMS ethic of examining our appropriate relationship to Mother Earth and the school's encouragement of exploration and community.

Assuming incorrectly that I would raise my children as my mother raised me, I learned there needed to be new ways. I learned this with both of my husbands and am grateful for the realization that our times require great tolerance and acceptance of others and the influence their particular history imposes upon them – sometimes without their knowing it. I struggle now to understand what my four adult children can learn to select and weave into their lives from the collective experience of our generation and do not want to be like the aspen tree roots which travel laterally and aggressively and drink more than their share.

Here I am with two of my grandchildren and I hope that someday they will know as much about this piece of machinery and those who used it as they might know of a rocket or a computer.

This year my roots are tangled with a passionate photographer who has helped me once again learn to love our landscape through the stories of our participation in it. She has asked us all to tangle up with her in that way. We will be the better for it and so will our children and friends."

"Here I am with two of my grandchildren and I hope that someday they will know as much about this piece of machinery and those who used it as they might know of a rocket or a computer."

Suzi Sewell

"The Sewell family has owned and operated their ranch in the Crystal River Valley for four generations. Suzi and her late husband, Bob, moved to the ranch in 1971. They raised their two sons there. Jason is now twenty-four and Alex seventeen. Bob died four years ago and Suzi is determined to keep the ranch for her sons. She and Bob, whom she considered her soul mate, used their talents, resources and just hard work to maintain the lifestyle they loved so much. She is pleased they were able to share the ability to work hard and the value of getting an education and seeing the world with their boys. They will need the resources to meet the terms it will require to keep the ranch for the future. New laws concerning inheritance and other tax laws have made it nearly impossible for young people to keep family farms and ranches.

Hard work and resourcefulness have kept the ranch alive, undeveloped, and beautiful. One limitation has always been water. Her husband's grandfather who homesteaded began with cattle, then with sheep then grew two train car loads of potatoes, but finally the water rights were sold and they could not afford maintenance on the ditch and now two hundred acres of the mesa is dry. Bob did not remember eating anything but mutton from the 18,000 head of sheep. They sent the lamb to Chicago because lamb was too expensive to waste on themselves.

"People who knew Bob thought he was an immaculate conception," she says. "All the parents did was work." After Bob graduated and he and Suzi were married, they returned from the service to the ranch to help his father. They started a business in Glenwood Springs. They began to look at ways they could keep the ranch together by setting up living trusts before their kids were born. They developed land. Bob went into construction. They leased their ranch in the mid-seventies. It wasn't paying its own taxes then.

In the early eighties, they bought a blasting company but all the work was in Hawaii due to a local recession caused by oil shale speculation. Suzi and the kids finally followed Bob to Hawaii where he worked for a short time. They were able to return and continue some form of ranching until his death.

Suzi hopes that by the time she is gone, growing hay and leasing for ranch projects will help the boys keep the ranch. She has encouraged her older son to get his education and travel now while he is young and unencumbered. Her trust in Jason is extended to his younger brother Alex and is implied in this advice. "Go see the world. Don't worry about jobs yet. Don't buy all the toys you want and go into debt now. Get out there and see the world." It should help them know what to do."

by Adele Hause
with help from Corinne Platt

"Hard work and resourcefulness have kept the ranch alive, undeveloped, and beautiful."

Louiva Stapleton

"I love spring, because everything is coming to life again. And I always say, 'If I live through the last of January I'm going to live to make it to dig in my garden, to plant.' And that's when I start buying my bulbs and things like that."

When I arrived at Louiva's, I found her sitting on her porch facing her garden, her granddaughter's ochre-colored puppy at play. Born in Collbran, Colorado and raised in Aspen, Louiva lived a hard but good life. Brought up without a mother or father, she is a self-made woman.

"I know once upon a time I didn't have any shoes. And now my family teases me about it. I made up my mind as a child that some day I would have all the shoes that I wanted. And I have them. They tease me about it now, 'So mom, how many pairs of shoes did you buy today?' when I go to Glenwood or something like that." I told them, I said, "If you'd been bare-foot, no shoes, you'd-a felt the same way I did."

Determined, independent and benevolent, Louiva has carved a niche for herself in a tight community of friends and family. Her love for children provides devoted companionship. In her home on 5th and Francis she showed me her photos on top of the piano. Generations. Louiva is proud not only of her own four children, but also of twelve grandchildren and eleven great-grandchildren.

"I feel like I'm very blessed."

"Between my heart attack and my cancer surgery, I had twin great-grandsons born. And I knew she (her granddaughter) had to have some help. So they were just the lift I needed. Just exactly what I needed. And I was at the hospital after they flew them back from Denver because they were very small, one weighed three and a half pounds and the other one four and a half pounds. I used to go up there and the nurse put a rocking chair in the nursery for me and she would say, 'Now you can take them out of the incubators and sit down there and rock them, do whatever you want to do with them. Just love 'em, that's what they need now.' So I did! They are almost nine years old."

by Molly Ogilby

"And I always say, if I live through the last of January I'm going to live to make it to dig in my garden, to plant."

Laurie McBride and her daughter Kate Puckett

"Two women: mother and daughter.
So alike, yet so different.

Alike, in that they are beautiful, energetic, full of joy and laughter, and share an extraordinary zest for life.

Not alike in that their zest, their love for life, manifests itself so differently:

For Laurie, it is expressed through her love of place – in particular her garden and flowers. Nowhere is she happier than with her fingers in the soil. But her love also shows up in a 'never-before-eaten' soup, or from the sound of classical music, or from the splash of a brilliant watercolor. All this, coupled with her deep caring for other individuals – especially one child at a time – makes her life as well as those around her a joy.

To have grown up in the logical and structured world of the east, and find yourself suddenly attached to the spontaneous, "always-in-the-present" world of Laurie is to indeed receive a daily potion of unpredictable and healthy medicine.

For the younger Kate, the zest for life may manifest itself in the 'whoosh' (and I mean 'whoosh') of a downhill run, the dizzying roll of an aerobatics flight, a well-planned devious, yet humorous prank, or a raucous, lusty laugh. Above all, however, her spirit is most readily seen when she works with cancer children from the Silver Lining ranch or the Sunshine Kids. Somehow, some way, her spirit and enthusiasm become theirs.

To be around Kate is to be in awe of what's growing in a garden you had a hand in planting. Energy, joy, enthusiasm coupled with organized efficiencies makes me wonder whether either her mother of I were the planters."

by John McBride, husband and father

"Nowhere is she happier than with her fingers in the soil."

Virginia Lappala

"My husband Paul and I came to Carbondale in 1971. Carbondale was full of stray dogs (they weren't stray – they owned people) and hippies who didn't want to get married and raise children and now they are pillars of the community. Wait until they write their book. They were my friends because there was only one person my age whom I met.

We had been attracted to this area by long-time exposure to the scenery and skiing and had acquired property that needed to be looked after. We shared many mutual interests besides our family of three: social work, peace building, civil and human rights, community development, environmental health, weaving, teaching, and travel.

My work has consisted of educational pursuits both giving and receiving. In Jefferson County I helped a homebound student who could not make sense out of letters. That was before we knew about dyslexia. When I arrived here and learned that Betty Grindlay of Aspen was teaching a course to help dyslexic students, I jumped at the chance to learn. It was the first time I had a "profession," the first challenge that I thought I had the skills to meet. She said I had a good "bedside manner." I continue to tutor dyslexic students. I have received inspiration and guidance in my informal pursuit of watercolor painting through CMC courses over the years. I'm still pursuing it.

Other interests: trying to keep fit – walking, biking, nordic skiing, aerobics. Advancing age requires more and more time devoted to such matters. I participate and volunteer in various senior projects, and find myself being very busy with the ordinary things of life – maintaining a house, yard, and car, being aware of what needs to be done – and doing it. Life adjustments will have to be made as eyes and ears grow dimmer, but so far I'm in excellent shape, and thankful to be so."

*"Carbondale was full of stray dogs, they weren't stray –
they owned people."*

Marcy Bayless Balderson and Polly Bayless Whitcomb

Marcy Balderson

“Looking at this picture of my sister and me, it appears like I have been through many a long, hard winter. In actuality, that is far from the truth. I have lived in Aspen for the summer, and at some point it will become the autumn, of my life.

Coming to Aspen from outside of Chicago thirty-eight years ago, it was as if I had died and gone to heaven. It was a combination of many things that I fell in love with – the openness, the freedom to be me, the friends I made, my sister living here as well, the skiing, the adventure of it all, and oh yes, the best part of all – meeting and falling in love with my husband! Colorado, this valley, and Aspen was for me a “Coming home” and to this day, whenever I return from somewhere, it is the same – ahh! Home sweet home! It is not just a mind thing, it is a real physical feeling, as my body feels and operates at its optimum here at this elevation.

So the “roots” started growing, children happened, and Aspen revealed another layer as a wonderful place to raise kids. They too grew to love the freedom and the mountains just as I had. This valley is changing, has changed, for that matter will always be changing, but I know that no matter what, it will always be a place I will carry in my heart emotionally, spiritually, and physically – it's called putting down roots.”

“...oh yes, the best part of all – meeting and falling in love with my husband!”

Polly Whitcomb

“I clearly remember the first time I saw a collection of old quilts. I was struck by the startling power, intricate stitches, and pure creative expression. It was fascinating to think of the homes of those 18th-century women as both studio and gallery and their quilts as examples of an art form that sprang from scraps of fabric and scraps of free time. Later I began to appreciate quilts as records of family history, as a treasury of American textiles and as a uniquely American expression.

I began quilting soon after I moved to Aspen in 1961. I find a balance between the freedom of the endless possibilities of color and shape and the discipline of measurement and stitchery. I prefer to make scrap quilts, using many pieces of fabric collected over years, featuring the greens, browns, and purples I see reflected in the mountains of our valley. Quilting is for me a kind of benediction and meditation.

Over my sewing table is a faded photograph of my great-grandmother, her sisters, and daughters all seated around a large quilting frame somewhere in Pennsylvania. Quilting is the link that connects me to them and to my past.”

“It was while I was a freshman at the University of Colorado that I drove into Aspen one cold January evening and felt that I had come home.”

Marie Maurin

"Marie Maurin was born in Neudorf, Switzerland on August 27, 1910. After spending her childhood in her native land, Marie went to England prior to World War II. She met her husband, George A. Maurin, in a pub, The Black Bear, in 1944; he ordered a sandwich and then asked to meet the cook. The cook was Marie, and when Mr. Maurin saw her, he said, "I'm going to marry you." And he did. They married April 27, 1944; two days later George was shipped out and they were not to be reunited until April 1946 at the Glenwood Springs railroad depot. He was transferred all over Europe for a year or so and ended up in a hospital in Paris for battle fatigue. He was sent back to the US without his Swiss wife and discharged in time for fall harvest and haying in 1945.

Marie's journey started in England where the war brides had to board a ship bound for New York. It continued by train to Glenwood Springs; however, her ticket's final destination was Emma, Colorado. When she finally arrived it was early spring of 1946 and plowing had already started on the Maurin Mesa-therefore no honeymoon!

She immediately took her place as a rancher's wife. George and Marie had to live with his parents until their own home was ready. Marie helped with all the daily activities that it took to run a large sheep and cattle ranch. It wasn't long before the footsteps of little ones came along. Dwight was born February 5, 1947 and his sister, Judy, was born thirteen months later on March 11, 1948. Marie had her hands full with raising two children, cultivating a garden, driving a stacker team, making clothes for the kids, baking, and studying to become an American citizen. Marie continued the tradition that Lillie Larsen Maurin began by selling farm fresh butter and eggs to select citizens and businesses of Aspen.

George and Marie enjoyed twenty-nine years of marriage before George passed away in 1976. Today, Marie has four grown grandchildren who greatly admire her for her fortitude, zest for life, tenacity, and strong religious faith. Marie just celebrated her 89th birthday with her family and friends. Marie has been a renowned baker, as any of her friends can attest. Her bread and pies were the BEST. Marie is like the Rocky Mountains that she loves so much. She has always been a source of strength and guidance."

by her granddaughter Laura Urban

"When she finally arrived, it was early spring of 1946 and plowing had already started on the Maurin Mesa – therefore no honeymoon!"

Ruthie, Ruth and Darcey Brown

"My earliest memories of Ruthie's Run in Aspen, which was named after my mother, was of "little Ruthie" sitting on my lap riding up old #1 (pictured). I was probably eleven or twelve and she was five or six and too small to ride alone. We would pull the heavy canvas cover over us, trying not to let the frozen lining touch us, and we'd peer out the plastic peep hole. We were always a little nervous that we wouldn't get the cover off in time to unload or that the gate on the chair would stick. Back then we knew all the lift operators and could usually count on Red Rowland being at the top supervising and unloading.

Ruthie's Run was named after my mother because she wanted an easier way off the mountain. At that time, the only way off was Spar Gulch, and it was a tight, gnarly gully. She put up some money and talked some other people into doing the same and had a new run cut. It was a great run, but the lines at the bottom of #1 were awful. We'd often wait for up to an hour. The lines would snake way up past the Skiers Chalet Steak House. My father threatened to permanently pull our passes if we cut in line so we never did. He was always a little tough on us, so we wouldn't set bad examples, which we probably did anyway. When Ruthie applied to be one of the first ski patrol on Snowmass (and subsequently had a run named after her as well), he told the area manager to "make damned sure" she was more qualified than the other hires.

We skied as a family a lot growing up and would often take spring picnics to Little Annies to ski. Despite the fact my mother helped build the Aspen Ice Rink we never skated much, although we did hike, camp, and take part in rodeos and 4H. Growing up, I didn't think my mother going elk hunting on horseback or ringing chickens' necks was unusual, but in retrospect it's astonishing, considering she was raised in the city by a full staff of servants and had very little experience with the outdoors or ranch living. I think what I admire most about my mother is her ability to enjoy and be comfortable with different lifestyles and people from all walks of life. And it's that same classless attitude that I admire most about the Roaring Fork Valley and hope can be preserved."

by Darcey Brown

"Growing up, I didn't think my mother going elk hunting on horseback or ringing chickens' necks was unusual, but in retrospect it's astonishing, considering she was raised in the city by a full staff of servants and had very little experience with the outdoors or ranch living."

June Kirk Crook Blue

"June's grandfather, James Madison Downing III, came to Colorado Territory from Iowa in 1872 as an Indian agent and returned in 1889 bringing family and friends. He settled the townsite of Clarence (now Marble) plotted in 1881. The hand-hewed log house beside Beaver Lake was one of the first and only remaining ones built at that time. June was born and raised in Glenwood Springs, and in 1943 she paid the taxes on the place back to 1923 and claimed possession of the property. Grandfather Jim was a guide when President Theodore Roosevelt came to Colorado to hunt bear and mountain lions near Marble. June's early memories are granddad's hounds baying in harmony. June's turn to greet a president came at about age five. She presented a huge bouquet of flowers to President and Mrs. Hoover when they came to Glenwood on the train. The president lifted her up to the back platform and helped her back to terra firma after she gave the flowers to Mrs. Hoover.

During her twenty-three-year marriage to Lloyd Blue whom she married in 1938, June moved forty-four times...more than Mamie Eisenhower. In 1945, they set out with their two young children for California to make their fortune. They rode the last train out of Aspen at Christmastime with a car full of Fritz Benedict's potatoes on the way to the brewery to make Spud Booze – a war enterprise. Twenty days later they were in Lewiston, Idaho, broke! They had fun anyway building and skating in the town's first roller skating rink. Lloyd also built houses, motels, schools, airports, and cabins.

She recalls the great Carbonate Creek floods of the 1941 and 1945. The '41 flood was first noticed by Anna Harris, the postmistress at the Williams Store. She heard and saw the mud coming down the hill. She phoned everyone who had a phone (actually it was all on one line). The Marble quarry workers were coming down on the electric trolley and saw it. Some of them jumped off and beat the trolley to the mill site. A wall of mud and boulders and trees was moving through the middle of town spreading out over three or four blocks bringing all of the debris. The first flood went through one door and out the other of most of the houses set North to South, filling them up with mud. As it came down, it took out the Main Street Bridge and flowed to the Bell Tower and Bandstand filling the bottom level of each. It spread out and turned Helen Williams' house and pushed it half a block off the foundation onto Silver Street. Later, the kids dug out a piano which still played. The 1945 flood came down Main Street toward Beaver Lake and cut a channel between her grandmother's house and her sister's house across the street. The huge trees her granddad had planted so many years ago kept it in line so it did not touch the Dowling house. This flood wiped out all the debris from houses being torn down or moved and filled the Crystal River below town. People were already moving away due to the quarry and mill closing as marble was not needed in World War II. They were leaving anyway. It just hurried them a bit."

by June Blue

"The first flood went through one door and out the other of most of the houses set North to South, filling them up with mud."

Isabel Mace with daughter Lynne

"There are many legends about the men who came to match our mountains, but when we wanted a woman – when we needed a woman – to match our mountains, the Goddess sent Isabel. Her soft voice and her small frame could not hide the power of her convictions and her commitment to do what was right while she was on this beautiful, small, and increasingly ailing planet.

Isabel came to Aspen in 1948 along with her husband, Stuart, to start a dog sled operation and to raise a family in rustic simplicity. They were pioneers of their time – as bold as the early pioneers in America – forsaking the promise of the American dream for a life more in harmony with the natural world. Theirs was the exploration for a truly sustainable lifestyle. Together they ran a restaurant, taught kitchen arts, used and taught about natural foods and organic farming, and founded a small farm school in southern Colorado. No wonder that they were among the world's best storytellers.

They raised a family of five fiercely independent children imbued with the pathfinder spirit, interested in alternative medicine, rare woods, organic farming, continuity of spirit and family, the gifts of ancestors, the individual, the land, the animals, the plants. Isabel and Stuart – in telling their stories by firelight, by sharing their home and their struggles, by living a wholistic life and thereby questioning the values of a confused world – were gently helping humans find their humanity and helping many of us re-shift priorities.

Together the Maces served as the environmental conscience of Aspen and as the stewards and spiritual conscience of the Ashcroft valley. They were willing to look head on at what the natural world was trying to say to us and were courageous in relaying the message of warning to the rest of us. They consistently did what we all know to be right – they gave more than they took.

As in the popular song "Evergreen," in which a member of a couple is characterized as a morning glory and the other is characterized as the midnight sun, so this couple complemented each other by adding either outgoing creativity or quiet steel to the union. One provided thrust – the other was a grounding force. They were business partners and lovers engaged in a well-choreographed dance with one providing the flourish of color and the other organizing and giving strength to the steps. While Stuart danced a rhythm as colorful at times as a combination of an Argentine tango and a Scottish highland fling, Isabel provided a uniqueness of rhythm which was as elegantly resounding, steady, beautiful – and as vital and life-giving to the dance – as a heartbeat."

by Susanne Caskey

"When we wanted a woman – when we needed a woman – to match our mountains, the Goddess sent Isabel."

Gretl Uhl

"Flavored by Bavarian design, the interior of Gretl's house is a gallery of handicrafts. All the cabinets in her kitchen, the chest in the living room and the chairs around the hospitable kitchen table were beautifully hand-painted by her husband, Sepp. Although there are many details to divert your attention, photos of Aspen's earlier days, works of art and knickknacks, you are pulled by the allure of the kitchen; it will fuel your soul. With a sweep of her hand, gathering the years, Gretl pronounces, "You wouldn't believe the people who have sat at this table, rich, poor, famous, small..." It doesn't demand such a stretch of the imagination, for no matter who you are you feel welcome and are immediately engaged in amicable conversation.

Most readily acclaimed for her restaurant on Aspen Mountain from 1966-80, Gretl's past is testimony of more than just one restaurant. It proves devotion to hard work and a pure, mountain lifestyle. Born in Bad Toelz, Germany, her upbringing included an education in fine cuisine from her parent's restaurant in the Olympic Skistadium in Garmish-Partenkirchen as well as a commitment to the German National Ski Team from 1941-51. In 1953 she immigrated with her husband, Sepp, and daughter, Renate, to Aspen. A year later her son Tony was born.

Committed to excellence, Gretl soon became the first woman to have top classes as a ski instructor on Aspen Mountain. Gretl not only made an impression on Aspen but she also discovered that she loved to teach. She found that she loved to "feel the people," to discover their idiosyncrasies and to try and reach them. She instructed for eleven years, becoming one of the highest paid instructors on the mountain and also serving three years as the director of the Rocky Mountain Ski Instructors Association. Her work as a ski instructor came to an end when one day she approached Corporation President DRC Brown and proclaimed that she wanted the next mountain restaurant that was built. In 1966 a restaurant was built and Gretl's stood until 1980 (where Bonnie's is today).

In every reference to her time running the restaurant, she claims nostalgically, those were "Happy Times." And in fact her restaurant was legendary, not because she sought attention, but because of the way she managed it. She explained that she can't do anything half-heartedly and that she expected the same of her staff... "We did so much, we gave of ourselves...we stuck together like glue."

At the time it was unheard of to find appetizing delicacies on a ski mountain, as is more common today, and it was Gretl's goal to pave the way and change the quality of mountain food. Everything was freshly made daily, from the spinach salad, to the strudels, to liver dumpling soup and breads. "You eat with your eyes," she explains. The menu was always in flux, often depending on the weather and based on requests. They never had anything left over. She claimed that some people would ski by in the morning with a note most likely written at home asking them to set aside so many strudels for their 2 o'clock lunch break.

Gretl's restaurant was people friendly and the food was the product of her passion. Magazines and newspapers from all over the nation and abroad celebrated her effort. When asked what her most successful attribute is she said, "I love to organize. I can walk into a place and see what needs to be done. The people who usually organize have no hands-on experience.""

by Molly Ogilby

"We did so much, we gave of ourselves...we stuck together like glue."

Margaret (Miggs) Durrance with husband Dick

"Nothing ventured, nothing gained."

I have no idea when my mother first uttered those words to me, nor how many times she repeated them, but they have guided me through life's choices for as long as I can remember.

She lived the words. As a girl she rode a family friend's horse to a national championship. As a young woman she ventured out to Sun Valley to try for the 1940 Olympic ski team. The games were cancelled, but she found a husband and cameras in a tree. (My father, famed ski racer Dick Durrance, who instead of training, was photographing the action from a tree.)

My father taught her how to work the camera. As they moved from Sun Valley to Alta to Aspen, she photographed her family as it expanded to include my brother, Dave, and me. More importantly, she recorded the evolution of those little mountain towns as they grew into world-famous resorts.

With my father, now a filmmaker, and on her own as often as her role as wife and mother permitted, my mother ventured out of the Roaring Fork Valley to distant corners of the world. She and Dad moved the entire family to Germany, where we lived for several years. Photographing alongside Dad, she traveled to Norway, Italy, Chile, India, Burma and Nepal. With assorted women friends she traveled to the Middle East, China and Russia. And on her own she rafted and flew into the Alaskan wilderness. It was a hunger for adventure that inspired her trips and her cameras that made them possible. Editors in New York and Washington published her pictures in *Life, Look, Sports Illustrated and National Geographic.*

In her willingness to venture forth, my mother made remote places seem close, and so, thanks to her, my brother and I never hesitated to travel far in search of our dreams.

by Dick Durrance II

"It was a hunger for adventure that inspired her trips and her cameras that made them possible."

Amelia Cullet Trentaz

"I have lived in the Roaring Fork Valley all of my life. I was born in Aspen in February, 1919, in a small miner's cabin in the east end of town. A friend of my parents was in attendance at my birth and she was the mother of Arthur, the man I married in 1940. So we must have met when I was very young. My father was always a rancher. He didn't own the ranches but rented them and grew the various crops. I had one sister eighteen months younger than I. I started school in Aspen as a first grader at the age of five. Living there in my early years was fun and it was a good life – very simple and Aspen was quiet.

When I was seven years old, my parents bought a small ranch at Canyon Creek, nine miles west of Glenwood Springs. Life in the country was good as we had good friends and neighbors. I went to Canyon Creek School, a one-room school. There were all eight grades and when the older children were giving their answers aloud, one could gather a lot of knowledge by listening. I received a good education and it was a fun time. When I finished the eighth grade, I attended high school in Glenwood Springs, and apparently the country school education was adequate as I had no problem adjusting. After graduation there, I attended Mesa College for two years and then transferred to Colorado University.

I married Arthur Trentaz in 1940 and became a rancher's wife. His family ranch was six miles north of Aspen. Ranch life wasn't always easy, but it was a good and rewarding life. We raised potatoes, cattle, hay and grain crops. Our two children spent their growing-up years there and were happy to be in the great outdoors with all that acreage to roam around in. We sold our ranch in 1962 and moved into Aspen's west end. It was quite a change for us. I really missed the great scenic views of all the surrounding mountains.

After our children were grown and in college, I got a job as library assistant at the Pitkin County Library. I loved the job. Being around and working with all those books and the wonderful people who read them was a great pleasure. I still love books and reading. I worked there until I retired in 1979 but I volunteered there until 1994. I volunteered at other locations all those years: The Thrift Shop, Museum and the Music Tent. I enjoyed the activities at the Senior Center. Life was good, fun and rewarding.

When we moved down valley to Glenwood Springs in 1994, it was sort of like coming home after all the years gone by. My sister still lives here which makes it very nice. The valley has been home all my life and it is still the best place to be."

"A friend of my parents was in attendance at my birth and she was the mother of Arthur, the man I married in 1940."

Betty Pfister

"Betty Pfister's life is characterized by a call to action. From the landing after her first plane ride as a young college student through much of the development of aviation, she has found ways to return to the skies. Those who fly in and out of Aspen, those whose lives have been saved from downed aircraft in the mountains, women pilots worldwide, Russian helicopter pilots, and all who can appreciate half a century of determination and adventurous spirit have Betty to thank. She is one of 172 recipients, eleven of whom are women, to receive the Elder Statesman of Aviation Award presented by the National Aeronautic Association in Washington, D.C. She has earned her place in the Colorado Aviation Hall of Fame and the Aspen/Snowmass Hall of Fame.

She was a twenty-one-year-old student at Bennington when she decided what she wanted to do with her abilities and skills. She told her parents she wanted to be a pilot. They could not have foreseen how far she would take this desire, but they struck a deal. If Betty stayed in college and kept up her grades, they would pay for her flying lessons. She not only did this, but graduated six months early to fly as a Women's Air Force Service Pilot in WWII.

When the war ended, there was a surplus of pilots in the job market. Betty felt lucky to find a job as a co-pilot for $3.00 an hour. The pilot sitting next to her was getting paid $5.00 an hour, and he was lucky to have the income. She bought a surplus P-39 fighter plane, named it "Galloping Gertie" (It is now in the Smithsonian Museum.) and entered air races and dogfights at shows everywhere. Over the years, she owned and operated eight aircraft, including "Tinker Bell" a beloved helicopter painted like a butterfly. She was Colorado's first helicopter pilot and she used it to help rescue downed fliers as well as to enter competitions. "I'd rather fly 100 hours in a helicopter than one hour in a plane." She later received her license as a glider pilot in 1966 and lighter-than-air balloon pilot in 1975.

The wedding of WASP friend Ruth Humphries brought Betty to Colorado where she met and married Art Pfister in 1954. Betty has changed the aerial culture in Aspen by lobbying in Washington to obtain an air traffic tower; planning and supervising construction and management of the helipad at the Aspen Valley Hospital - the first in Colorado - and founding Pitkin County Air Rescue in 1968. She has been very supportive of other women pilots. Five years ago she learned of the Night Witches, Russian women who flew night missions in defense of Moscow during World War II. (They do not like this name given to them by the Germans.) She had studied Russian and found one of them and paid a visit to learn of their experiences. "They were up there all the time, in combat, while we were just flying across the country." Her support of other women pilots has included being president of the "Whirly Girls" and sponsorship of several Russian helicopter pilots. (Much of this material is from an article by JoAnne Ditmer in an article published in the *Denver Post* October 13, 1994.)"

by Martha Lorch and Adele Hause

"I have more of a fighter plane spirit that (that of) a bomber."

Mirte Berko, her daughter Nora Mallory and granddaughters Mirte and Eliana Mallory

"Together we are named after a white Italian flower. Together we plant the yearly blossoms of color. Together we eat cookies, together we drink four o'clock tea. Together we laugh about the way life used to be, together we sit, my Omi and me.

Flower planting, weeding, plucking, and seed collecting are not to be overlooked at the Berko's turquoise-gray Victorian. June finds us sitting on low benches under the swaying pine tree as Omi reminds me how to arrange the petunia roots so they grow thick and resilient to the Colorado extremes. Watched intently by glistening eyes, I combine the proper proportions of old and new soil and alternate the color selection. Omi remembers the colorful petunias she first saw upon arriving in a deserted Aspen. She's begun a family tradition and soon my younger sister, Eliana will join and help us under the shade of generation-old trees.

July, and the banister disappears beneath a sea of purple, pink, and white. Ready for lunch, I anxiously await the fire station's twelve o'clock siren and pluck the petunia's dead heads. Oh no, my bike-grease-covered hands are no way to treat these precious plants. Omi hands me the scissors and shows me how to cut them just so. Today the daisies at the wrought iron gate call for weeding. We disappear beneath a blanket of white trying to distinguish between the good and bad green. I am reminded of Opi's photograph of abstract winter fences. Omi's harmonious voice takes me back to her childhood and the gardens in which she played and danced. I smile with delight.

August. The petunias are even fuller and bow the banister. The daisies have been cut. Today we collect columbine seeds to plant next summer. Omi's long delicate fingers have no trouble opening the thin brittle pods. I find the task more of a challenge. Under the rustling lilac bushes and the chokecherry tree we dry the seeds in rows on soft paper towel. With smiles and a bit of coaxing, Omi laughs and tells stories about the old Jerome pool in the summer and the wide dirt streets. I strain to hear the bleating of sheep through town.

Mirte and Mirte, two unique flowers, two different generations with different yet echoing aspirations. Mirte and Mirte, united by the traditions of family and of place. Each year I look forward to my flower days with Omi; a sanctuary of ritual and grounding hidden in the heart of our rapidly changing town. Like Miss Rumphius, Omi has gone to faraway places and come home to live in the mountains. She has also done something to make the world more beautiful. Through flowers and stories Omi has planted and helped grow seeds within me which are anchored in the past and propel me with wisdom and tradition to continue to spread color. Now, as the next Mirte, I will follow my grandparents, but as for making the world more beautiful, I do not know yet what that can be."

by her granddaughter Mirte Mallory

"Each year I look forward to my flower days with Omi: a sanctuary of ritual and grounding hidden in the heart of our rapidly changing town."

Gladyce Hart Christiansen and daughter Joyce Christiansen Kearns

"Two pioneering women, mother and daughter, grounded by a ranching life.

When I asked Joyce what characteristic she thought best defined her mother, "a lady" was her response. "She loved to shop, and it was exhausting to try and keep up."

Even today she is a true lady, polite and cordial. She was always active in Aspen society. Pictures of her early days exhibit her elegant beauty; she was known as a femme-fatale.

Gladyce Christiansen was born November 25, 1911 in Aspen. Her mother's uncle was one of the first thirteen prospectors to come to Aspen. He homesteaded up Capitol Creek, where the St. Benedict's monastery is now, and acquired the land by trading $5.00 and a pair of rubber boots. Her grandfather, Fred Hart, is credited for naming Hell Roaring Creek. Gladyce grew up on the Hart Ranch and attended the Capitol Creek School on horseback. She fondly remembers the country dances, where she danced the fox trot and waltzes and met her husband, Jens Christiansen. In 1932 they were married, and Gladyce moved to the Glendale Stock Farm on Owl Creek which Jens bought with his father in 1924.

In their living room in Glenwood Springs Joyce and Gladyce have a painting by Joy Caudill of the Owl Creek Ranch. It portrays the idyllic beauty of western life, both romantic in its landscape and realistic in the work it demanded. Life on the ranch called forth strength of character and independence. From Mary Hayes' book *The Story of Aspen*, Jens is quoted, "When we threshed, all the neighbors would come to help and my wife, Gladyce, and mother, Sophia, would cook meals for about twenty men."

Joyce was born August 19, 1934 in Aspen and lived twenty-one years on Owl Creek. She attended the Owl Creek School and claims that she was a tomboy. Jens used to run the cattle up on high government ranges in the summer. When I asked Joyce if she worked right out there with him, "Oh yes." was her response. By the age of six, Joyce worked alongside her father leading the stacker horse, while Gladyce, who had grown up with four brothers, favored the indoor chores. Joyce recounts that her mother could saddle a horse because she rode, but she was never a tomboy like me.

Joyce claims that her upbringing on the ranch proved useful to her as a military wife. Her family moved often, and her husband was away for months at a time. Her self-sufficiency and independent nature allowed her to adjust and manage on her own. Other wives, she said, were fearful and helpless without their husbands."

by Molly Ogilby

"He homesteaded up Capitol Creek where the St. Benedict's Monastery is now, and acquired the land by trading $5.00 and a pair of rubber boots."

Corona
Extra
LA
CERVEZA
MAS
FINA

The Sandoval Sisters
Margaret Gallegos, Rita Bejarano, Becky Hutton and Dolores Montoya

"Our roots began in a valley much like the Roaring Fork Valley, Taos, New Mexico. A mountain softer looking than Mt. Sopris but just as beautiful was part of our early years. Our father (an engineer and surveyor) for the highway department brought his six daughters and five sons to Colorado in 1940. He left behind an adobe house with three large rooms and two acres that he sold for $1200 three years later. The family is many many generations from New Mexico and Colorado on my mother's side as well. There are now thirty-seven grandchildren, seventy-three great grandchildren, and twenty-five great-great-grandchildren. We gather once a year for a camp out at Wellington Lake. We all know each other.

We sisters enjoyed living in that adobe house that our father built by himself. The house was filled not only with his eleven children but numerous visiting cousins. It seemed that one of our aunts was always visiting with their children as they lived within walking distance. Growing up in a small town in a large family taught us many domestic traits – from washing diapers in cold water to cooking Sunday dinner. The house chores were divided up, which instilled the sense of helping others. The work of doing chores was thought of as just a part of everyday life. It was easy to enjoy the chores since there were so many others who would enjoy the end result. Because our mother did all the cooking, it was left to the children to keep a clean house, do the laundry and tend the younger siblings.

As is well known, the Latino culture celebrates many festivities within the families and with the community. Therefore, there was many a time when the 'tamale-making party' was on, and again everybody had their chore to do. Some of us were spreaders of the dough on the corn husk, washers of the corn husks, rollers of the husks once they were filled (In those days they were tied at both ends with a thin strip of corn husk!).

The older, more-experienced sisters made the chili and the dough and kept the bowls filled up. Also there were the ones who did the more mundane job of cleaning up. Perhaps it is this cooperation and training that has brought us all to do the jobs we do in this valley, providing domestic services to those who call on us."

"...there was many a time when the 'Tamale-making party' was on..."

Beulah Wilson and her granddaughter Erica Weaver

"We were very much in love," Beulah Wilson said when asked why she ventured this far west from her home in Shenandoah, Virginia. Her first child, Annie Wallace, son Bailey, and daughter, Virginia, were all born at home in the Roaring Fork Valley. Old Doc Tubbs delivered them all. Beulah remembers that when she first went to Doc Tubbs with morning sickness and he diagnosed her as pregnant she didn't know what that was. "My mother never talked about anything," she said. Virginia explained that in those days one said, "The Stork is coming."

"We worked very hard," Beulah said, confessing that for a woman who didn't know how to boil water, when she arrived, she learned to cook – for her family and hired men. She also learned to hoe a garden, sew, quilt, and can. "I canned the loveliest cauliflower. No one had ever heard of it being canned." She helped take care of the young community, helping with the library, fire department, church community basement, hospital, medical clinic, and the Near New thrift store. She also worked for public welfare, the Garfield County office, for twenty-four years first as a caseworker and then as a director.

Her husband Bailey lived until 1945. "He was a perfect husband and father," Beulah said. "She knew how to pick good men," Virginia added. Two-and-a-half years later, Beulah married Bailey's distant cousin, a sheep man, John Wilson. "John Wilson always brought his 'bummers' down to us to take care of," Virginia said. "While mother was married to Daddy, a cattleman, she ate beef. When she married John, she switched over to lamb quickly." John Wilson lived until 1977.

Beulah remembers when John and Anne Holden came to found the Colorado Rocky Mountain School on the Prideaux ranch across the river. "They worked morning to night and didn't take time to cook," she said. "So, many nights they came to eat with us. They were wonderful people."

by Adele Hause

"I canned the loveliest cauliflower."

Winifred Conway Rector

"Very little remains of Perin's Peak, the mining camp above Durango where Winnie grew up. She was born in Walsenburg in 1916 to Scotch-Irish parents and graduated from high school in Durango. She knew lots of mining families and was happy to marry a cowboy, Bill Rector. They lived on a ranch in Rangeley and had three daughters and a son.

In 1960 the Rectors moved to Carbondale to live on a ranch on Missouri Heights. Winnie's main loves in life were her family and her church. She was not a "joiner," but nothing was too much bother to do for her children. She used to drive to school to get her kids and take them home for lunch. Some special memories for them include how much she relished playing April Fool's jokes on her family and how she insisted that sweet peas be planted on St. Patrick's Day.

Arthritis hit Winnie seriously after the birth of her last child, but determination kept her going. She would sit and crochet with her curled-up fingers fighting to keep them useful. "Where there's a will, there's a way" was the motto she lived by.

It's a good thing Winnie isn't writing these comments, because she never knew the most important thing about herself: the inspiration and joy she gave to others. Despite her arthritis, severe pain in her later years, and finally amputation of both of her legs below the knee, Winnie managed to spread cheer and to focus on her friends. She was about five feet tall and weighed about ninety pounds, but her spirit was enormous. To watch her manage to live at home alone, getting around on her electric scooter, was a powerful example to all who knew and loved her. Winnie passed on the legacy of honest hard work and pride in her own traditions...a combination which serves to nourish the human spirit. Carbondale lost a wonderful lady when Winnie died in 1998.

"Where there's a will there's a way"
written and sung by Tracy McLain

She said I don't know what I'd do without you
or how I'd ever make it through.
I was thinkin' that I should be thankful
for the privilege of knowing you.
She's in those later years when the days can get
real long.
She likes it when I sing my song.
She showed me the meaning of a friend.
I know I will never meet a soul like her again.
She has the strength it takes to make it all this way.
She's never given up.
She knows there's a brighter day.
She's strong and kind and you don't know
when you might find the next angel in your life.
She sees the beauty in the smallest things.
She hears angels when I sing.
I watched her struggle and I heard her pray.
She said where there's a will there's a way.
She has the strength to make it all this way.
She's never given up."

by daughter Jillene Rector

"...she insisted that sweet peas be planted on St. Patrick's Day."

Mary Eshbaugh Hayes with daughter Bates

Mary Eshbaugh Hayes

"Coming to Aspen in 1952 to be a reporter-photographer with *The Aspen Times*, I had the good fortune to work for owners Ruth and Verlin Ringle who were well-liked in town and who knew everybody (there were about nine hundred residents then). They introduced me to everyone and Ruth told me tidbits about many. I decided Aspen was filled with colorful characters.

Mr. Ringle was publisher-editor and he and I did all the writing for the newspaper. Ruth ran the business office and Elmer Peterson was the linotype operator. We were the whole staff. (Now there is a staff of some sixty.)

In addition to gathering and writing the news, one of my jobs was to write the "10 years ago, 25 years ago, 50 years ago" column. I was fascinated with the stories in those old papers. On quiet afternoons, I would wander around town and photograph the old Victorian buildings.

After Jim Hayes and I were married in 1953, I was able to stay home with our five children for some eighteen years. However, except for five years when the children were little, I have written the "Around Aspen" column every week from 1952. Starting a small photography business in our home, I did photographic portraits of many of my favorite people and did photo stories for *The Aspen Times*, and many weddings.

I wanted to put photographs of these wonderful people and scenes around town into a book and came up with the idea of a cookbook titled "Aspen Potpourri." which I published in 1968.

Going back to work on the newspaper in 1972 as a reporter-photographer, and then as editor, I found my greatest interest was in the history and the people of Aspen. Each week I would try to research and write an historical article or do an interview with someone.

Most of the time, staff photographer Chris Cassatt and I did these stories together and for years we talked about putting them into a book. After semi-retiring in 1993, I began work on "The Story of Aspen: The History of Aspen as Told Through the Stories of its People" which we published in 1996.

Covering the events and news, taking photos every week, talking to all those people and writing about their weddings, their births, their joys, their tragedies, their life stories and their obituaries – I hope I have helped preserve and become part of the history of Aspen.

Bates Hayes

The joy of living in a place like this is that its context constantly shifts. Having been born to this place, I have no sense of how it used to be or what it will become. I have always viewed it as living at the Carnival. The characters change, and the place changes with them. Growing up here I have lived in so many different towns and experienced so many different lives – each passing with the bittersweet ending of a fairy tale, never to be had again. The difficulty of living in a place like this is that in your heart, you can never quite find your way home."

"... I would wander around town and photograph the old historic buildings."

Ruth Whyte

"I have enjoyed my involvement with the Aspen community and its people and I feel very fortunate to have my permanent and only home in this beautiful mountain setting of Aspen during the latter part of my life. So in between my personal life of running a home, taking care of a dog and sometimes other people's dogs, managing two rental units, gardening, my photograph hobby, skiing, hiking, tennis, entertaining, attending many of the wonderful cultural events, having house guests, and traveling, I will continue to be involved with Aspen community services as long as I can. A short review of some highlights:

My arrival: I arrived in Aspen in January 1952 with Bunny Whitaker in my Nash Rambler from Kenosha, Wisconsin. I worked three or four jobs and changed housing three times, then broke my leg in February.

My turning point – May, 1956: The National Ski Association Convention was to be held in Aspen over Memorial Day weekend and I ended up organizing the meetings at the Jerome Hotel and the events because those ski club members who bid for the convention had left Aspen.

More packing up: I became Executive Secretary of the Aspen Ski Club in the fall of 1957. With Jack Carson, president, I helped set up an office in the front of *The Aspen Times* in a space donated by the new editor, Bill Dunaway. From 1957 to 1966 we were constantly packing up all the office gear to store it during the summer and then proceeding to find new office space from October to April.

I had so much fun: As secretary I coordinated the training schedules, the coaches, the housing and meals for teams from Canada, Iceland, and Chile. These smaller teams so appreciated our efforts that I went to see them at races in Squaw Valley and Sun Valley. I have fed the Canadian Ski Team and staff every year since 1957 except for one year when I was ill. What a fun and appreciative group. In 1970 I decided to donate my frame house on Second and Bleeker to the Aspen Ski Club for its permanent home.

I ran into a tree: In April 1981 after a very serious accident and three operations lasting into that summer, I desired to seek more volunteer involvement.

It was a "win-win" situation: In 1990 I coordinated with the C.U. history department and Foundation to set up the Roaring Fork Research Scholarship Fund for the purpose of annually selecting a C.U. history graduate to do summer research on a certain aspect of Aspen or Roaring Fork Valley history. The society gets in-depth history on mining, ranching, and skiing factors and the C.U. interns, giving credibility to their portfolios.

I have with pleasure opened my home: I have enjoyed hosting many for meetings, meals, and housing to the Aspen Ski Club, Race Officials, the Aspen Historical Society, C.U. research interns, actors with the Aspen Theatre in the Park, entertainers for the Wheeler Opera House Associates, Music Festival students and faculty, Aspen Writer Foundation guest writers, Winterskol guests, and of course to my family and friends from all over the world."

"I will continue to be involved with Aspen community services as long as I can."

Betsy Schenck

"I was born in Denver and schooled at the University of New Mexico and at Colorado College. I always wanted to go east to finish my study of piano. So when I got accepted as an artist-student with Wolfgang Rose in New York City, I began arranging my farewell concert for my pupils and myself in Denver. At the recommendation of Wells Music Company, I called the private Jewish club, The Town Club, in the mansion of Mrs. Crawford Hill and talked to the manager, Mr. Robert Schenck, to see if their beautiful facility and grand piano (it only looked grand, I found out later) would be available to a gentile like me.

Bob Schenck came from upstate New York to go to the Hotel/Restaurant School at Denver University. After my summer of study which was to have led to a Town Hall recital, I married Bob Schenck (Mr. Rose never forgave me for abandoning that project.) and we moved to his next job in Texas where I found my darling babies under the cabbage patch. It was a big surprise to me to find myself in such a situation – a mom! When they all grew legs and personalities (they grow in spite of everything you do) we found ourselves looking out at Mt. Sopris from our place on Missouri Heights.

Somehow, I became a board member of the Crystal Theatre, and at one of the meetings I was asked if I would like to teach piano and voice for the new Colorado Mountain College. What a wonderful odyssey that became! I was teaching voice, piano, chorale, music appreciation, drama, opera, all with practical productions attached. I became director of the Bach Chorale and Kinderchoir but doing "Carmen" on the stage of the Crystal Theatre has to be the pinnacle of my very illustrious career. It was just a fine way to utilize a twenty-six-foot stage. I wonder how the stage of New York's Town Hall compares – 126 or 226 feet? I do know that the diameter of the rose window in Paris' Notre Dame Cathedral is twenty-six feet.

After retiring from teaching, life has sent me many blessings. I got to meet a fine cardiologist in Grand Junction and a fine violinist whom I get to accompany from time to time. He is the artist-in-residence at Colorado Mountain College, Bob Yang. He is going far.

I'm not meaning to upstage my own six wunderkinder and eleven grandchildren who are making fine contributions to the world we live in. My husband Bob and I manage our properties and a small herd of canines and one idiosyncratic cat while we visit our families from time to time. St. Barnabas Episcopal Church in Glenwood Springs is my sole venue for singing and playing these days plus an occasional concert in my own living room on my own truly grand piano. You're invited. Bring cookies!"

"What a wonderful odyssey that became!"

Susorine Diemoz Bon and Mary Diemoz Glassier

"We didn't have money to buy skis, but dad made old clumsies (sleds) when it snowed. We'd go up on the hillside clear up on the ditch and we'd coast down over the rocks and down that little hill. My brother and I would go up there after school. We'd fall off. Got hurt a few times. It's very different from what the kids do nowadays, I can tell you."

Mary Glassier and Susorine Bon's parents immigrated to Leadville from Italy. Susorine was born in Leadville right before her family moved to Marble, where Mary was born at the Prospect Ranch. Their oldest sister was born in "the old country," Italy. Later, their folks bought the Ranch at Roaring Fork for what they think was about $3000. "I came down from Marble when I was three months old in a lumber wagon. I don't remember much," Mary chuckles.

The girls went to school at the Catherine School. Mary went to high school for a month but had to quit when her folks needed her help on the ranch. "Believe me, as soon as you were able to do something, you worked. We didn't have all the modern things kids these days have. We didn't have refrigerators. You had an icebox if you were lucky or you'd put it down the well. Dad had an ice pond. We'd cut big pieces of ice, shoe a team of horses, and get the ice loaded on a wagon, then get it to the storage room and cover it with sawdust."

Susorine remembers wanting to play ball down in Carbondale, but it took too long to ride her horse down there from the ranch and too much time away from working on the ranch. Their dad had an old Model T Ford that both girls learned to drive. They both remember lots of young people in the valley, but not much of a social life. Maybe a picture show once in a while. "When we were kids, we didn't go any place. Whenever we went anywhere, we had to have a team of horses and a spring wagon."

She also remembers going to Glenwood when there used to be places to tie your horses. We occasionally went to the Glenwood Hot Pool though we never quite learned to swim. "You could do quite a bit with a nickel in those days. Carbondale had the closest grocery store. We didn't buy much there, maybe coffee and macaroni, not even flour. They took the wheat from the ranch to the flour mill in Glenwood and traded it for flour. When you had to have some meat, you just went out and knocked a rooster in the head, and that's how you got your meat. We never went hungry, that's for sure."

by Corrine Platt

"When you had to have some meat, you just went out and knocked a rooster in the head and that's how you got your meat."

Louise Jackson

"She had four daughters and she was always supportive of anything and everything we wanted to do. I never heard, 'Oh you're just a girl. You shouldn't do that'," Sandy, her youngest daughter told me.

Louise didn't stop at raising and encouraging her own daughters. By the end of our interview, it was clear she had influenced, encouraged, and, in part, raised hundreds of girls. Her dedication began in the sixties with her Girl Scout and 4-H involvement in the Roaring Fork Valley. Today she no longer co-leads trips into the Colorado wilderness, Minnesota boundary waters, Mexico, across old wagon train routes, or on ocean schooners out of Seattle; rather she makes her contribution to the Girl Scout board and hosts a camp each summer on her four-hundred-acre ranch. When she isn't serving the Girl Scouts, one might find this beautiful seventy-four-year-old at a Friends of the Library meeting, teaching a student through the adult literacy program, helping with the Garfield Youth Services newsletter, or working in the Lift-Up office.

She and her husband Carter live in the home they moved into thirty-eight years ago. They met on a dude ranch in Wyoming. She was a guest and he was a wrangler going through veterinarian school. After falling in love, they decided to share the rest of their lives, and they moved to Fort Collins, Colorado. Louise taught chemistry at CSU for a year while Carter completed his studies. Soon after, they moved to Glenwood Springs with their first daughter, Thersa. They lived next to the vet clinic for the next ten years where they grew to a family of six. Nearly fifty years later they have four daughters, seven grandchildren, and a life well-rooted.

Four daughters, seven granddaughters, and a mom who never said "never" makes for a family with a lot of girl power and female energy. Louise Jackson doesn't call herself a feminist or activist or volunteer her talents for any other reason than that she wants to leave the world a better place, although she is the first to admit: "It's been good to us."

by Martha Lorch

"I never heard 'Oh you're just a girl. You shouldn't do that'."

Lee Ann Eustis with a Colorado Rocky Mountain School crew

"To me there is still such a heart to this valley. I feel that there is a core here of real spirit. There is a way of life and a way of seeing that I try to keep with me when I'm not here."

Lee Ann came to Colorado with her husband George in 1960. "He took this silly Philadelphia girl west of the Mississippi to a waterfowl refuge in Monte Vista, Colorado." Lee Ann left a successful career in advertising and publishing and never once looked back. She attended Vassar College and sees it as a wonderful irony that she found Kit Strang, a Vassar graduate, five minutes away from her in Carbondale. The two of them raised their children together and are lifelong friends. She and her husband George dedicated their lives to education in the Roaring Fork Valley. He taught at Colorado Rocky Mountain School and the Aspen Country Day School, and Lee Ann served on both boards and loved to tutor young "bad boys."

"Sopris is my spiritual focus in life. In my younger days, I looked at it as more of a playground. One of the first things we did with our kids was attempt to climb it. But now it is my spiritual focus. To my children it is also the focal point they always come home to." Every time of the day Sopris looms large out of the many windows in Lee Ann's home on Missouri Heights.

"When George died unexpectedly and the children were so young, there was no doubt in either family's mind that I would go back east to finish raising the kids. It never even crossed my mind to leave here. It was a pure feeling that this was my home. I belonged here. Our house up on the hill was a mecca for kids and music and friends. I think what is unique about Carbondale is that there is such a diversity of ages and lifestyles. Back in Philadelphia, I couldn't have a best friend who was twelve years older or younger than I am.

"Here people are supportive. These surroundings have made me appreciate the special aspects of being alone. My times to take that symbolic deep breath are just so in tune with nature and this countryside. That is my story of the West."

by Corrine Platt

Fortunately for me, Lee Ann loves music, just as she loves lots of people and many diverse things. And she loves the arts in general – boy, howdy, does she love them. Countless hours spent crisscrossing Colorado for the planning session, the symposium or just another meeting have borne wondrous results. If anyone thinks it's an accident that the Carbondale Council on Arts and Humanities was given the Governor's Award in the arts back a few years ago, he or she can meet me in the parking lot later and we'll discuss it.

A tribute by
John Robin Sutherland,
friend and pianist for the San Francisco symphony.

"To me there is still such a heart to this valley. I feel that there is a core here of real spirit. There is a way of life and a way of seeing that I try to keep with me when I'm not here."

Marlyn McCrady Fiscus

"Marlyn never said times were hard as I talked to her. She commented that her children, grandchildren, and all of the students from Colorado Rocky Mountain School are doing things you could never imagine. Her life is also unimaginable in some ways.

Her parents moved from California to New Raymer, Colorado to Farson (Don't blink!) Wyoming. By that time, she and her husband had joined her father in setting up a machine shop near the Hiawatha Oil Camp near Craig, Colorado. When they saw an ad from the Federal Land Bank for two hundred acres in Spring Gulch (now an area of nordic trails leased from the local cattleman's association), they came sight unseen to the Roaring Fork Valley. "After the Depression and the Dust Bowl in eastern Colorado, it was like heaven! There was a good house, a barn, a windmill – and the well never did run dry." They raised what they could to eat. "I always said, eat what you can and what you can't we'll can." They brought some Herefords from Wyoming. They tilled the field and planted brome grass. They bought a baler. Later they planted the land to fall wheat. One year they got sixty bushels to the acre. They took a five-gallon can of cream to sell to the Glenwood Creamery once a week. They also did some custom bailing for other ranches, one of them the Mulford Ranch which is now the Ranch at Roaring Fork. They lived on the Spring Valley Ranch for fifteen years – and had electricity for about half of the time. "My grandmother had died and left me a small inheritance and so I bought a Queen motor-driven washing machine right away!" They also had a cook stove and a Warm Morning – a cylinder you could put a bucket of coal in to heat the house.

Marlyn and Lyle and their four children left Spring Gulch as Lyle became ill and they had to sell the stock to pay the hospital bills. His parents could no longer take care of the place and so it was sold. Just then the survey crew was working to open the Coal Basin mines. Marlyn and Lyle moved to Redstone and lived in a little trailer where she would cook the workers a dinner. Lyle would load the horse into the pickup, put the hot dinner in the cab, drive as far as he could, unload up the horse, and take the hot meal to the survey crew.

And then the Colorado Rocky Mountain School opened in 1953 and was lucky enough to find Marlyn to be the chief cook. She stayed until her retirement in 1998."

by Adele Hause

"I always said, eat what you can and what you can't we'll can."

Ruth Brown Perry and her daughter Rosamond Turnbull

"I was born in Denver at the end of the First World War in the midst of a devastating flu epidemic. I had a wonderful childhood with three older brothers and a neighborhood full of children. Bob Perry and his family lived close by on Eighth and Grant. His grandparents lived on Grant, had a stable and kept their horses there. Bob's grandmother drove her horse and buggy downtown on the gravel streets to the market. Bob rode with his father and grandfather often to Cheeseman Park and around that part of Denver.

Bob always knew he wanted to ranch and started working on one when he was fourteen. I loved to ride and be in the outdoors, and we both loved to ski and to race (he far more successfully than I). We married in our early twenties and lived in Steamboat one year. Then we had an opportunity to come to Carbondale which was small like Aspen and had a wonderful ranch that was in sad shape. The three-story ranch house was built in 1907; it was in dire need of repair. Chickens had been kept on the second floor, and old vegetables and rotting fruit on the third. A light bulb swinging from a cord in the living room was our introduction to our future home. I had a kindergarten on the third floor of our house for several years. There was one church, the Community Methodist Church.

We took four or five boys in the summertime to help with the haying, some from the East, some from the West and even a few from England and France. It was a busy ranch life with our seven children. In 4H the youngsters did plays as well as showing horses, steers, heifers and lambs. We did lots of riding, hunting, skiing and trips with family and friends.

In the early 1950s John and Anne Holden came to see us to talk about school locations. They finally ended up purchasing the Bar Fork, thus Colorado Rocky Mountain School was born. I served on the board there, the public school board and the church board in addition to teaching Sunday school for twenty-five years.

I have been very blessed with Bob, family and friends and to have lived in Colorado and the beautiful Crystal River Valley. It was such a wonderful place to raise cattle, horses and children with "God as our refuge and strength." Psalm 46:1"

"I have been very blessed with Bob, family and friends and to have lived in Colorado and the beautiful Crystal River Valley."

Ruth Brown Perry

"When we look into the faces of our mothers, we see them not just as we know them now, but the reflections of their years before we were born. I see my mother as a fearless young bride, elk hunting with my father, her hair flying as she holds her rifle steady at a full gallop! You still feel twenty inside when you are eighty but you've learned a lot. We all have roots holding us in place and whether this has been your home for 100 years or 100 days, you can feel the magnetic pull of this valley on your heart.

My mother's family has been here for five generations, roots sunk deep in the soil with years of stewarding the land, raising families, building community and friends. She grew up riding her horse in the hills around Aspen and passed her love of the outdoors on to her children and grandchildren. Her great-grandchildren are old enough now to see the high-country lakes she rode to with her father.

I am so grateful for my mother. She has taught me so much about giving, friendship, joy, enthusiasm, zest, perseverance, faith, hope, and most of all, love. She lives her favorite verse, "Trust in the lord with all your heart and lean not on your own understanding; in all ways acknowledge Him and He will make your paths straight.'"

I see such beauty in my mother's face. She lives life to the fullest and I'm grateful."

A tribute by Rosamond Perry Turnbull

Jane Hendricks and her daughters, Harmony, Hillary and Heidi

"I was born in the dirt. Have enjoyed wiggling my fingers and toes in it all my life. I come by it honestly. My ancestors grew tulips in Holland and migrated to Kansas where they hoped to have some space and not have to spend all their energies draining the land. Hardly our problem.

I'm a farmer. (Agricola, agricolae and all that.) I like to grow things that feed me and the other creatures who dwell here with me. I need to feed the body and the soul, the goats and the geese, the birds and the bees (all 120,000 of them), the worms and other critters of the soil, the startling inhabitants of secret places, snakes and spiders. I don't love them all. You can have the wasps and the grasshoppers.

I have one of those gardens only a mother could love. Too tall flowers, awkward and leaning. Gone to seed. Hardy annuals. So reliable – they come back every year – even where you'd least expect them!

My garden's reassuring to me. Seeds are a promise and a miracle. "The seediness of things," as Neva Daniel would say. Snakes and spiders make me feel that all is well with the world. I take repose by watching bees or simply walking around my yard. I do love fresh spinach, mind you. But I reap a lot more than that. I love my yard."

by Jane Hendricks

"I have one of those gardens only a mother could love"

Elect
BRAD HENDRICKS
Good enough for government work
ETY4870
COLORADO

Heidi Hendricks and *The Gros Ventre Gazette*

"Beyond the Power Lines"
Excerpt from *The Gros Ventre Gazette*
by Heidi Hendricks, founder, publisher and editor

"Duane Kramer came up here yesterday and in passing conversation mentioned that he thought he might have been born 100 years too late. It's a popular phrase out here. Seems like I've heard it a bunch. I think I've even said it myself a time or two, That the West, the real West, the wild West, was finished long before now. Was gone with paved roads, barbed wire, power lines, concealed weapons acts, progress, progress, progress. I have had silly visions of myself free and uninhibited. Horseback in Irish Canyon. Coming up to Wyoming to see my man. Before the days of cars, roads. Just me and the West, bra-less and bad. But a person forgets. I wouldn't have been bra-less and horseback anywhere 100 years ago. I would have been corseted up as some man's wife or whore.

People lament over what is lost and even I, when I go back to Colorado, can get depressed. Woe is the cattleman whose son is selling highballs out of a drink cart on a golf course that used to be his ranch. But let none of you be mistaken. The West is still here. There is still land. So much land. Rejoice that you can still get lost. Would you believe that people still shoot at people's feet and tell them to "Dance or get the hell out of here?" That people tie their hands to saddle horns thirteen miles from home "cause they're so drunk and it's so dark, and it's blizzarding so hard that if they fell off they'd be coyote meat." People still rope bears. Walk ten miles for one measly Bloody Mary. Dive over bars and into liquor shelves head-first. Trot thirty miles on a horse with a broken leg! Climb a 12,000 foot mountain to slide down on a trash bag cause there is no TV to watch. No computers to play on. I've seen a man grab a hold of a tow rope behind a snow machine and on skis, shit-faced drunk, two in the morning, get towed fourteen miles going eighty miles an hour. That was pretty western!

That there are still places that you can truthfully say that you would kill or die for every single person within a thirty-mile radius. And that's not even the land. What about the land? The valleys leading into valleys leading into valleys. Creeks and rivers and cliffs and forests and that is just what I can see from my window. There are still places where you are so alone, so alone that you go outside and scream, and nine times out of ten a dozen coyotes will answer you. Reassuring you that you're not really alone. I can go on all day. Didn't want you people up North, down South, back East to worry. There is a place that is the West and it's still pretty western."

"There is still land. So much land. Rejoice that you can still get lost."

RED'S
ISLAND

Peggy Cooper Rowland and her daughter Roine St. Andre

"When I was a child I could ride from my grandfather's house anywhere. He had a drugstore on Hyman Avenue, and I could go up there and tie my horse and go in and talk with him. Can you see me riding up Main Street and over to Hyman Avenue now on a horse?"

Peggy Rowland laughs as she elaborates on a lifetime in Aspen. "...I'm blessed. I tell people that I was born here, and they think 'she doesn't know up from down.' And then I tell them that my mother was born here and that my granddad had a drugstore here and my father had a bookstore here originally."

Peggy has lived in Aspen on and off for eighty-four years. Though she and her husband Red raised their four children in Aspen and Peggy became an integral part of the community, life in Aspen, in the beginning, came at a price. When she was a child, her father struggled to make ends meet and their family moved to Denver. Later she and Red also left due to economics. "His self gave out and we came back in the spring of 1946. We moved into his home which had been vacant for ten years."

"Well, I cried when we moved back here. I'll be real honest. We didn't have a job and had four little children. I sat with the twins – they were six months old – in a chair and cried and cried. I thought, where are we going from here? Red put up ice the first year we were here. And then that next year they asked him to bring material up for the sun deck on Aspen Mountain. He had an old truck he drove up with the lumber and what not on it and then they asked him if he'd like to work when they built the lifts. So he started at the bottom at the Aspen Skiing Company and then he ended up as the vice-president in charge of construction. He loved that! He loved being outdoors, he was not a man that would have done well in an office. He worked hard, not much pay in those days. We got the house put back together gradually, a lot of hard work...beautiful wood work, I loved the woodwork in that house. I saved dimes for furniture. I got two nice chairs back then, one of them is up in our cabin now."

Facing Red's Island in the Roaring Fork River, Peggy is perceptive about the changes occurring in the natural world. "No, it's not a bad place to live, nothing really terrible happens...we did have a flood here after a heavy winter, and due to the heavy run-off the river changed its course."

by Molly Ogilby

"I cried when we moved back here. I'll be real honest. I thought 'Where are we going from here?'"

Barbara Snobble

"The last thing in the world I thought I would become is a "pioneering" woman. I figured my ancestors finished that in the 17th Century. As a progeny of Chicago, Vassar and New York, I thought I was headed for law school, the State Department and archeology.

Imagine my shock finding myself in Carbondale in 1954, a nondescript village off a dirt highway with none of the amenities one expects of small towns, such as village greens, parks, trees – and at the beginnings of Colorado Rocky Mountain School, which had minimum facilities itself. (Each spring, the well went dry; each winter the shower became a glacier; cloth baby diapers took four days to thaw and dry on the line.) But here I am still.

My first encounter with the West was in 1947 after I joined my fiancé and we drove to Aspen – a town on the verge of changing from a defunct mining town to a world class ski resort. The town was full of old mines, educated ski bums, and mountain troopers. This is where I learned to ski on Roch Run and the Corkscrew; we had the original ski wedding that spring...a story in itself!

My real western adventures began in the summer of 1947 when with my husband we climbed the Tetons, horse packed in the San Juan mountains, visited the New Mexico pueblos, fiesta-ed in Santa Fe, rafted rivers, explored canyons, and camped in mountain meadows. It was my Epiphany. The beauty, cruelty, vastness, variety, the unknowableness of the Rocky Mountain West captured my heart and soul.

The appeal of the Roaring Fork-Crystal Valley came later, the complete geology, irrigated fields, mountain meadows, sage flats, rocky slopes, caves, mines, woods, grazing cattle, sheep, horses, deer, elk, lions, bears, coyotes and smaller beasts and the delightful mix of people – ranchers, miners, teachers, merchants, farm wives (real pioneers) plus the varied personnel of the Colorado Rocky Mountain School from everywhere else, all of them with their own lore and lives to share.

Also I remember my sadness when Ray Fender's potato fields were first bulldozed on the way to becoming what is now known as Crystal Village. Bit by bit we have lost all that hard-won valley land and surrounding mesas to highways, housing developments, and commercial growth; now the mountain forests are filled with hikers, bikers and motorized recreationalists.

While I have traveled most of the United States and much of the world indulging my interests in old history, this valley is still my heart and home.

I am so thankful for my life here with my husband, children and friends. The deer still frequent the lawn although horses have gone, and I continue to hear the ever-changing sounds of the Crystal River and see the eternal presence of Mt. Sopris and the Red Bluff from my windows. I would not change it."

"The beauty, cruelty, vastness, variety, the unknowableness of the Rocky Mountain West captured my heart and soul."

Emma Danciger

"When I look at the mountains surrounding our Colorado ranch, I understand what the Psalmist meant... "looking to the hills to gather my strength."

I am amazed to find myself here – a gal from Mississippi enjoying the best years of my life in the shadow of these mountains.

My ancestors were farmers and merchants. Some were seeking refuge in America from the oppression of Europe, others were immigrating from the British Isles to the golden promise of America. They made their way down the eastern seaboard to merge as my family in Mississippi. My grandparents continued to farm, raise livestock, and run businesses. When they moved to "town" they continued to nurture the land and the community. Some cared for others as county clerks and sheriffs.

From my grandmothers, I learned to love home and hearth. I learned those skills of gardening and cooking, quilting and needlework. The most important lesson I learned from my namesake, Emma Crane Thompson, was there was always room for one more at the table, in the home, and in the heart.

Our small family unit came to Colorado about thirty years ago. We finally brought cattle from our Texas ranch about twenty years ago. We love and respect the land and are honored to be guardians of what we have.

I express myself with my fiber arts. Quilting connects me with my past and has given me an avenue to the future. In addition to making new quilts of contemporary designs and re-creating traditional patterns, I have great joy in restoration of old family quilts. I feel so lucky to rescue a family treasure keeping memories alive.

The stories quilts tell are of the women who helped settle our great land. Their toil raised food, children, and hope. Their devotion gave love, nurture, and beauty. Quilts signified birth, lifetimes and death and hold all those memories for years to come.

I will try my best to tell those stories and teach those skills to my grandchildren and the children of my wonderful community and home – Carbondale, Colorado."

"Quilts signified birth, lifetimes and death and hold all those memories for years to come."

Connie Harvey, Dottie Fox and Joy Caudill

Joy Caudill

"I look back over the years and see how much this mountain environment has affected my life. The way we brought up our children was influenced by this special place we live in. We did a lot of camping, hiking and skiing as a family. I wanted our children to experience the same intimacy with the natural world that I had known as a child. It was a gift my parents had given to me.

My love for the wild high country has caused me to become deeply involved in wilderness preservation. I paint watercolors when I get a chance, usually of mountains. I try to capture the seasons, the moods, and even the feel of the air. I paint other subjects but I always come back to the mountains.

These mountains have given me so much. They are part of me. I am not whole when I am away from them. I would rather sleep on the ground by a high mountain stream than any place else in the world.

Here in Colorado, wilderness is high mountain peaks echoing the rolling thunder of a mountain storm; it is a cold crystal clear steam tumbling down through the rocks and wildflowers; it is the fragrance of the fir trees and the clean smell of the air after a shower; it is the scream of the mountain lion, the bugle of the elk or the cheery song of the white-crowned sparrow. In the freedom of the wilderness we can live by the rhythms of the earth and not by the clock, giving us time to think, time to really see things – time to really understand the world."

"In the freedom of the wilderness we can live by the rhythms of the earth and not by the clock..."

Dottie Fox

"Being a native Coloradan, my love for this land has always been with me and for the past thirty years, my roots have been in the Roaring Fork Valley. Three of my four children, a son in Crestone, Colorado, and two daughters in the valley share my roots. I have hiked the trails, climbed the mountains, painted the landscape and worked very hard to protect this incredible place I call home.

To know that one has made a difference in saving little bits and pieces of the planet is the reward that keeps one doing environmental work, and the great people you meet who are doing the same thing makes it all worthwhile. My love for the land extends into my paintings of landscapes, animals, birds, and beautiful vistas. As my left brain deals with environmental issues, my right brain paints the lovely areas I try to save. It's been a good mix."

"I have hiked the trails, climbed the mountains, painted the landscape and worked very hard to protect this incredible place I call home."

Connie Harvey, Dottie Fox and Joy Caudill

Connie Harvey

"This is the story of the Aspen Wilderness Workshop and how it connects our lives. It began with two neighbors who wanted Congressional designation for the Maroon Bells-Snowmass Wilderness.

Before Congress passed the Wilderness Act of 1964, about half of what is now the Maroon Bells-Snowmass Wilderness was already called by that name. Hiking, backpacking, riding, ski touring, and other forms of "primitive recreation" were allowed there, but mechanized travel was not. Foot trails could be built, while logging, roads, dams, power lines, ski areas, and man-made structures were excluded. But at that time "Wilderness" was a Forest Service designation that could easily be reversed. It really does take an Act of Congress to keep the "wild" in wilderness.

In a famous introduction, the Wilderness Act of 1964 described Wilderness as land that is "untrammeled," where "man is a visitor who does not remain." Once given this designation by an act of Congress, the law requires preserving it in its natural state. All other public lands, such as national forests and parks, are subject to various kinds of development.

Joy Caudill and I were next-door neighbors and friends, and our children were playmates. My husband Harold and I bought our Maroon Creek property from Joy's parents, the Maxwells. We were drawn to its natural setting of beaver ponds, spruce, aspen, cottonwoods, willows, and wildlife. Joy shares my feeling for such places, so we joined forces in our very first forays into environmental activism.

We assembled some knowledgeable locals who shared our values. Together we studied topographic maps and marked existing and proposed wilderness boundaries, taking care that they made sense in the real world. Once satisfied with our work, we filed maps and a letter explaining our proposal with the Forest Service, and were soon lobbying Congress and local officials for our cause. We learned to write letters to the editor, attend hearings, and stay abreast of environmental issues. Our informal group became more sophisticated. To strengthen our power, we incorporated, built a membership, and held meetings. Soon after we had done that, Dottie Fox arrived on the scene and immediately became a very strong and dedicated leader, first forming a local Sierra Club group, and then joining forces with the Wilderness Workshop.

The Workshop led the fight for local wilderness, and eventually we had great success. Maroon Bells-Snowmass was made wilderness through an act of Congress, and its size more than doubled. Hunter-Fryingpan, the Collegiates, and the Elk Mountain Wilderness were other nearby areas approved by Congress over the years, and while we were not alone in working for this, we were the main grassroots group. We formed coalitions with state groups such as the Colorado Mountain Club, the Sierra Club, Western Colorado Congress, and the Colorado Environmental Coalition. We also worked with national groups like the Wilderness Society, the American Wilderness Alliance (now American Wildlands) and others.

We don't always agree with the Forest Service, but we make it a point to know our local Forest Service personnel and work with them when we are able. A joint project of long standing is our air and water quality monitoring program. A particulate sampling station on Aspen Mountain includes an automatic camera that takes daily pictures to create a record of visibility. That relates directly to the Wilderness Act, which requires maintaining the air quality of a "Class 1 Wilderness" like Maroon-Bells-Snowmass. Without the record we are making, this law could be hard to defend. Similarly, each spring and summer we sample the waters of selected high mountain lakes to measure changes in acidity. In recent years we have been making observations of exotic weeds and damage to trails and camp sites.

To protect the minimum stream flow in local rivers, we monitored water use in Snowmass and Maroon Creeks, and forced the Aspen Skiing Company to back off from a water grab in Snowmass Creek. That took heavy-handed persuasion – a lawsuit in fact – but we did reach a reasonable settlement.

The Aspen Wilderness Workshop has enlarged its scope to include the White River National Forest. The White River Forest Plan is being revised, and we are active participants. Logging and mining were once the main enemies of forest integrity, but motorized recreation is the greatest threat today. Illegal construction of motorized trails by off-road vehicle (ORV) and snowmobile users is devastating to wildlife habitat, and can be a death sentence to endangered species. We have proposed a travel management plan that limits ORVs to designated areas, while keeping other trails just for hikers and preserving critical wildlife habitat. Unfortunately, the ORV groups, heavily subsidized by manufacturers, have become a very powerful lobby.

Over the years, we've been called everything from "little old ladies in tennis shoes" to "eco-terrorists." But the Sierra Club honored us as "environmental heroes."

From being an all-volunteer group, we have grown to having some professional staff. As long as natural areas exist, groups like ours are needed to defend them. We have found many like-minded friends through the years, and it's wonderful that many younger people feel as we do.

For all of us, Dottie, Joy, and myself, what matters is that as much as possible of our immeasurably beautiful landscape and its native creatures shall be saved. The best times are those spent away from politics and paperwork, up in the mountains drinking in clean air, blue sky, scenery, sunshine and wildflowers. Or skiing through woods, or watching a water ouzel dipping in a stream or a red-tailed hawk floating on a thermal, or a doe with new-born fawn, or a hummingbird. Or camping out under a brilliantly star-studded sky, or zipping up under a gathering storm, far from home but close to nature, with all its wonderful sounds, sights, and smells, a priceless legacy we must preserve. ”

"Over the years, we've been called everything from 'little old ladies in tennis shoes' to 'eco-terrorists.' But the Sierra Club honored us as 'environmental heroes.'"

Jody Caudill Cardamone

"I am imprinted by mountain streams. They flow through my life defining different segments. Native to the Roaring Fork Valley, I was born on March 19, 1953 in the old, red brick hospital on Hunter Creek. For the first year of my life, I lived with parents and grandparents in the big log house looking out on the beaver ponds of Lower Maroon Creek. My grandfather, Roy Maxwell, would take me on his shoulders to feed the fish or cast a fly out into the pond to hook a trout for dinner.

When my parents' house was finished, like beavers, we moved across the stream. River sound dominated my world as a child, always whispering, splashing or roaring through the edge of my consciousness – a continuity and a strong presence which I miss today when not near water. I spent hours fly fishing in the big hole in the back yard, even singing all of my favorite folk songs to entrance the fish and charm them into rising to the fly. I was sure it worked.

Summers, my family of seven, including two younger sisters and two younger brothers, would spend every weekend camping. We returned year after year to sites on Lincoln Creek, East Maroon Creek, and as we got older, backpacked into most of the drainages that fed the Roaring Fork. Many we considered our secret places; the names held magic for us. It was our wild kingdom.

Leaving for four years to complete a BS in environmental education at Cornell University in upstate New York, I returned with husband, Tom, in 1975. We became acquainted while hiking the trails of the Hunter/Fryingpan drainages, completing a wilderness inventory sponsored by Colorado University in 1972, and we were married in the summer of 1974 on the banks of Maroon Creek. Back in the valley I became the first Director of the Aspen Center for Environmental Studies (ACES), incorporated in 1969 as an educational non-profit organization, through the vision of Elizabeth Paepcke. Located at Elam Lake on the Roaring Fork in the curve of the old glacial river bank, I found myself establishing roots only several hundred feet from where I was born. Soon Tom was hired and we became a Director-Naturalist team on twenty-five acres in the heart of Aspen. Today the river sound still runs through my consciousness lending the reassurance of continuity to our lives. Our two children, Kate, eighteen and Will, fifteen, born in Aspen Valley Hospital on Castle Creek, have become even more intimate with the water as ardent kayakers.

After twenty-six years at ACES, I feel how the power and beauty of the Roaring Fork watershed with its myriad of drainages has fed into my life and my imagination, like a giant placenta, nurturing, supporting and allowing my roots to go deep.

Although the degree of development and change has been overwhelming and painful at times, I realize this valley flows in my blood and I will continue to love it and call it home."

"I am imprinted by mountain streams. They flow through my life defining different segments."

Bleu Stroud

"My brother Emerald had been camping in the Marble area for years. During a visit he talked my husband and myself into a reconnaissance tour of his beloved Marble. The only person living in Marble was the county road maintenance man who kept the grader on the first floor of the abandoned bank building and lived on the middle floor of the three-story building. We rented a cabin from the only couple living a mile above Marble and immediately fell under the autumnal spell of the upper Crystal Valley. My husband, Howard, and I spent Christmas of 1956 there and purchased our present property, naming it Snowshoe as we had to wear snowshoes to see it. We lived in a tent the first summer with our two Manx cats, consistently rescuing them from being "treed" by the local wildlife.

My favorite activity was to fix a peanut butter and jelly sandwich in the morning and just hike all day, not being absolutely sure of my location, but always feeling that the mountains were friendly. I gradually became familiar with the maps of the area and favorite camping spots evolved as high in the mountains as I could manage. For winter camping we had skidoos to negotiate the snow-closed jeep roads. I enjoyed winter camping before it was "cool." A favorite place was under a huge spruce tree with its lower branch tips tied into the snow, forming a cozy tent all around. I shared it with a resident porcupine several times.

We had a prodigious garden for canning and freezing. We hunted elk each fall and bought a lamb from a sheep man. We picked wild serviceberries, chokecherries, and currants for pies, jams and sauces. I developed a passion for mushroom hunting and one year I froze over 200 pounds of different varieties of mushrooms.

I shared the same passion for learning about wildflowers, wild plums and wildlife, welcoming even dandelions to sunshine each spring. I had a love/hate relationship with raccoons that constantly raided my bird feeders. In winter I habitually put out extra hay when I fed the horses; a cow elk would be watching me from a short distance. This continued for several generations. Close encounters with bears were common and some were downright humorous, but I never lost respect for them.

Often I was lucky enough to catch a fleeting luminous alpine glow high on the peaks. The snow would become deep magenta when struck by shadows of cobalt blue. I walked backwards to watch my tracks fill with blue shadows. The hardest part of camping was coming down off the mountains.

I had studied painting in California and I continued to paint after moving to Marble, exhibiting my work in Glenwood Springs and the Redstone Inn. When Colorado Mountain College was being formed, I was asked to teach. As a continuing education instructor, I became familiar with every church basement, unoccupied office, school cafeteria or unused art room from Basalt and Glenwood to Aspen and Carbondale.

During good weather, classes were held outside on hilltops, riverbanks, or farmyards.

I have been a charter member of the Glenwood Springs Art Guild since its formation thirty-five years ago. I've witnessed it grow from a small group to being a real force in the art world of Colorado and beyond.

As president of the White River National Forest Association from the early 1970s to 1996, I felt honored to have helped facilitate the United Ute Pow Wow in Glenwood Springs in 1993. This was the first time in 135 years that all the Utes reunited. They came from Utah, Arizona, and New Mexico as well as Colorado. It was a time to remember with awe and deep respect.

I shall never hear a horse or sheep bell without memories of Ida and Elmer Bair's high mountain sheep camps flooding back. Over the years Elmer taught me so much about coping with the intricacies of mountain survival. We opened winter-clogged ditches in spring, and Elmer showed me the proper way to control spring run-off and repair where needed, how to assemble a pack train and load it, then how to move it out and keep it under control. I visited their camp often and especially remember Ida's busy, busy pressure cooker doing its thing on the sheep tent stove at suppertime, and Elmer's blackberry jam atop a slice of home-baked bread. I reveled in listening to anecdotes and personal recollections as only Ida and Elmer could tell them. It was pure joy with many belly laughs and "lessons in truth." Thank you, Elmer and Ida. ”

"I walked backwards to watch my tracks fill with blue shadows."

Afterword

I have always been fascinated by pictures that tell stories, or groups of pictures that suggest a narrative. This collection of photographs of women from the Roaring Fork Valley fulfills the promise of rich and satisfying story telling.

I appreciate photographs that stand on their own, that don't need an explanation. Photographs that one can just look at and enjoy and help you to make up your own story or narrative. Meredith Ogilby has beautifully allowed this to happen with her sensitive portrayal of these women. She knows them, understands them, appreciates them because she is one of them. Only an insider could give such an intimate view of these women and their histories.

I spent much time looking into their faces, examining the fragments of their room interiors, their clothing, the landscape they stood in. I wanted to come to know them first through their outward appearance. Being a visual person, I tend to trust my visual instincts first. So what did these pictures tell me? These women were strong, independent, hard working, serious but with a sense of humor, loving, connected, committed to the land, had a love of animals, nature and the outdoors, had faced hardships and endured, and left a legacy for their friends, family and community.

I then read their own stories, their words, to compare my own feelings about who these women were with what they told me about themselves. Not surprisingly, their stories did match beautifully with my imagined histories.

The collection of these lives, these anecdotes, tells us much about the influence of a place upon the people who choose to inhabit it. It also conveys something of women in particular, and their influence on place and surroundings. I firmly believe that "place" has a profound effect on the people who live their lives there. The Roaring Fork Valley, with its magnificent natural beauty, its rural atmosphere and western heritage, inevitably will mark the inhabitants. How different these lives would be had these women been living in New York City or Los Angeles, for example.

I am grateful to Meredith Ogilby for sharing her vision, her knowledge, her love of these women with us. She has allowed us to visit, inhabit and experience a segment of life in this country that many of us would never have access to. The journey has been exhilarating, enlightening and memorable.

by Judy Dater
Berkeley, CA

Judy Dater, a native Californian, studied photography at San Francisco State University where she took her M.A. degree in 1966. Dater has been the recipient of two National Endowment for the Arts Fellowships (1988 and 1976), a Guggenheim Fellowship (1978), and the Dorothea Lange Award (1974). Her work is housed in many prestigious collections including those of the Metropolitan Museum of Art, The Museum of Modern Art, New York and San Francisco, The Center for Creative Photography in Tucson, and the International Center of Photography in New York. Her publications include: "Cycles" *(1992, Kodansha Ltd., Tokyo), and* "Cycles" *(1994, Curatorial Assistance);* "Body and Soul: Ten American Women" *(with Carolyn Coman–1988, Hill and Co., Boston);* "Judy Dater: Twenty Years" *(1986, University of Arizona Press);* "Imogene Cunningham: A Portrait" *(1979, New York Graphic Society, Boston); and* "Women and Other Visions: Photographs by Judy Dater and Jack Welpott" *(1975, Morgan and Morgan).*

Acknowledgements

I deeply appreciate the encouragement for this project. The Colorado Council on the Arts and the Carbondale Council on Arts and Humanities (CCAH) provided initial grants. I was most honored to receive the 2000 Caroline Bancroft History Award from the Colorado Historic Society. The Aspen Historic Society and Megan Harris helped with broad exposure to the local community throughout an entire year. The Women of the West Museum and Director Marsha Semmel welcomed the project and reinforced the concept of personal story. Colorado Rocky Mountain School and Valley Folk Arts hosted the initial exhibit. Community was further built by others who hosted exhibits: the Wheeler Opera House, the Adelson Gallery of the Aspen Institute, Colorado Mountain College, Marilyn Murphy and the Gordon Cooper Library, Jane Hart and the Avon/Beaver Creek Library, Pam Eschenbaugh of the Irma Stein Memorial Library in Presque Isle, Wisconsin, the annual fund-raising dinner for CCAH in Six89 Restaurant of Carbondale, and Regina Kirby of Cattails Restaurant of Eagle.

Without the technical assistance of Scott Chaplin who helped with grant writing and Scott Gerdes of Colorado Mountain College and Brian Winters of Walnut House Photography, Jim Kosinicki of Carbondale Printing and Copy, Stew Eves of Eves Print Shop in Edwards, Sally and Frank Norwood of Main St. Gallery, Meg Bernet and Mike Horn, owner of Master Framers in Vail, and Susie Darrow and Linda Halloran, Mary Eshbaugh Hayes and Anita Witt for their publishing experience I could not have proceeded. I thank Sam Abell and Leah Bendavid-Val of Santa Fe Workshops who provided inspiration and direction in "Publishing the Photographic Project." I especially thank Brent and Barbara Bingham of Photo Effects of Edwards for the extra time and brainstorming far beyond photo scanning. Without the commitment and generosity of my dear friend, Joanne Morgan, and the loving attention to layout and design she gave this book, it would not have been much fun. I am honored that Betsy Marston and Judy Dater provided the Foreword and Afterword.

I feel fortunate that the following journalists recognized the value of this project and gave it visibility: Donna Daniels of *Glenwood Post Independent*, Judy King of the *Valley Journal*, Carrie Click and Donna Dowling of *Colorado's Roaring Fork Sunday*, Steve Lipscher of *The Denver Post*, Hilary Stunda of *The Aspen Times* and Marka Moser of the *Vail Trail*, Grassroots TV and KSNO of Aspen, and Jeannie McGovern of *Sojourner Magazine*. I also thank Molly Beattie of Alpine Banks who plans on book-signings and exhibits upon publication.

We thank the following people for their support, friendship and advice: Pat Fender for suggestions and hours of proofreading, Roz Turnbull for her patience, generosity and encouragement, Ruth and Darcey Brown for introducing me to everyone at the Wienerstube, or so it seemed, as possibilities for my project. Thanks to Ruth, I began a relationship with the Aspen Historic Society. I thank Corinne Platt, Suzanne Caskey, Judy Gold, Barbie Christopher, Darcey Brown, Martha Lorch and Molly Ogilby for their interviewing and writing assistance. What fun I had with Adele Hause who assisted me in many of the aspects of this project and provided copy and editorial help.

Thank you, Chuck Ogilby, for living and breathing this project without complaint over the past three years.

I thank all the featured women I photographed, we interviewed, visited with so many, many times, for your patience, good humor, faith in the project and most importantly, friendship!

Biographies

Editor's Note

Please enjoy the short biographies which we have collected. Some of the women preferred to let the short essay characterize who they were and preferred not to expand on biographical details.

Marcy Balderson was born in New Britain, Connecticut in 1941. She attended college at the University of Arizona for three years and then in Vienna, Austria for one year while traveling as much as possible. She moved to Aspen in 1963 and has lived there since with her husband, Herb, and two children, Dylan and Erica. They spend about four months every winter in their home in Costa Rica. In Aspen, she first worked as a waitress at the Crystal Palace, then had a business making one-of-a-kind children's clothes. She still works part-time as a seamstress. She has been involved as a volunteer for nearly twenty years with the Aspen Thrift Shop and various other charitable organizations giving time as well to the community in Costa Rica.

Rita Bejarano was born in 1946 in Taos, New Mexico and has lived in Carbondale for thirty years. Rita worked at Colorado Rocky Mountain School for thirteen years and was a cook at The Midland Café in Basalt for thirteen years. She is a widow with two sons and two grandsons. Her husband Larry was a barber in Carbondale for thirty years.

Mirte Berko was born in Berlin, Germany in 1914. After having lived in Paris, London and Bombay, Mirte and husband/photographer Franz, came to Aspen in 1949 and settled in the West End of Aspen. Mirte and Franz raised two daughters: Nora and Gina. While Franz continued his photography both locally and internationally, Mirte supplied Aspen with European toys through her shop The Toy Counter. Mirte continues to live in Aspen as do her daughters, sons-in-law, and five grandchildren.

An Aspen native since 1949, Nora Berko and husband, Howie Mallory, have raised four children in Aspen. Her youngest daughter, Eliana, keeps her very busy. After attending Oberlin College and studying in France, Nora lived in New York City until she returned to Aspen. She then taught French and German at Aspen Country Day School.

Mirte Mallory was born in Aspen in 1980. Having lived in France and New Hampshire, where she attends Dartmouth college, there is some magic force that pulls Mirte back to Aspen: it is home. Mirte cherishes the endless stories her grandparents have shared about old Aspen and their adventures around the world.

Eliana Mallory was born in 1995 in Aspen. She is a jubilant five-year-old who loves to travel and play travel agent. She is happiest when brother, Linden, and sister, Mirte, are home from school to take her skiing.

June Kirk Crook Blue was born to Elsie Downing and Henry Kirk of Marble in 1920. She was raised by John and Hannah Crook in Glenwood Springs from the age of fifteen months due to the death of her mother. She married Lloyd George Blue in 1938 at the Blue ranch at Catherine. Their first son Todd was born in the old Cheese Factory between the Roaring Fork River and the Catherine Store. June and Lloyd were married thirty-nine years until Lloyd's death in 1977. She lives in Marble when she is not visiting her family and is pleased that now the Marble school has reopened as a charter school and that the quarry has reopened to produce the stone that has enriched buildings worldwide through the past 119 years.

Susorine Diemoz Bon was born in Leadville in 1909 to Ernest and Rosina Diemoz who immigrated from Italy. After graduating from high school in Carbondale, Susorine began teaching at Catherine Schoolhouse. She also taught at the Missouri Heights and Emma Schoolhouse. She attended college in Gunnison in the summer. She married Arthur Bon in the late thirties and they ranched for eleven years until Arthur died as a young man. She lived in the home her husband built in Carbondale until the year 2000.

Ruth Brown was born in 1920 in Denver. After graduating from Finch College, she moved to Aspen where she owned and operated a small shop. During World War II, she served as a pilot in the WASPS. After the war, she raised five children and three step children on a ranch in Carbondale.

Darcey and Ruthie Brown are fourth generation Coloradans. Darcey was born in 1948 in Glenwood Springs and Ruthie in 1955 in Denver. Darcey received her B.A. from Wells college and M.A. in History from the University of Colorado. She taught and worked in Admissions at Colorado Academy and at Colorado Rocky Mountain School. She also was the Executive Director of Leadership Aspen. She is married and has two boys. Ruthie is also married and has two children. She is a graduate of Colorado Rocky Mountain School and the University of Alaska. Ruthie competed nationally and internationally in several sports and is now the coach for the Aspen Nordic Ski Team. All three serve on numerous regional and local boards.

Jody Cardamone was born Jody Caudill on March 19, 1953. She was the eldest of five wild redheads in the house designed by her architect father, Sam Caudill. She graduated from Aspen High School in 1971 with the questionable distinction of having invited Edward Abbey as graduation speaker. (Several parents walked out.)

She received an M.S. in environmental education from Cornell University. She and her husband, Tom, have two children, Kate, eighteen and Will, fifteen.

Joy Caudill is a third-generation Coloradan who grew up in Denver until the United States became involved in World War II. Her father signed up as a major in the air force and the family spent the next three years at air force bases in Lincoln, Nebraska and Ogden, Utah. Then, after V.J. Day, it was home to Denver where Joy finished high school. The family moved to Aspen in 1946. This was the year the first lift was built on Aspen Mountain. The family helped build their own house, a couple of cabins, and finally a studio for making ceramics. Joy and her parents developed a line of handmade and custom designed plates, mugs, tiles etc. called Aspen Craft. Their personalized pieces were created for people from all parts of the country. Joy married architect Sam Caudill six years after moving to Aspen. They have raised five children, four of whom still live in the valley. Joy has spent the past thirty-plus years working on wilderness and public lands conservation. She and Connie Harvey were founders of the Aspen Wilderness Workshop.

Margaret Dunand Cerise was born in 1918 in Italy six months after her father left for America. In 1929 she came with her mother and brother to Leadville, Colorado and met her father for the first time. She was six months old. She married Mela Cerise in March 1932 and they lived on their farm until he passed away in 1972. They had three children, Reno, Telio, and Lola Mae Russo who passed away in 1993. In 1979, she moved to Basalt where she continues to bake her own bread, keep an immaculate house and lovely yard.

Gladyce Hart Christiansen was born in Aspen November 25, 1911 to Fred and Ella Colby Hart. Her childhood years were spent at the Hart Ranch on Capitol Creek, which is now the location of St. Benedict's Monastery. She earned a teaching certificate at the University of Colorado and taught at the Upper Capitol Creek School for two years. She married Jens Christiansen in 1932. They owned and operated the Glendale Stock Farm on Owl Creek where they remained until 1990. Gladyce died in her home on July 22, 2000. She is survived by her daughter Joyce Kearns of Glenwood Springs, two grandchildren, and three great-grandchildren. She was a sixty-six-year member of PEO, a fifty-six-year member of Eastern Star, and a longtime member of the Aspen Literary Club.

Emma Elizabeth Alvis Danciger was born December 26, 1938 in Oxford, Mississippi. She attended Syracuse University and Texas Tech and was a pre-med major. She and her husband, David, have four children and six grandchildren. She enjoys gardening, especially flowers, writing, tennis, golf, and hiking. She is active with the Roaring Fork Hospice Co., Carbondale Senior Housing, Colorado Rocky Mountain School, the Aspen Deaf Camp, the Aspen Chapel and Aspen Jewish Community, the Roaring Fork Valley 4-H, American Angus Association and is a co-founder of Valley Folk Arts.

Neva Daniel was born in 1910 in Marceline, Missouri. She graduated from Ottawa University in Kansas and went on to teach at the Peddie School, Orme Ranch in Arizona, Colorado Women's College, Otero Junior College, Adams State College and for twenty-five years at Colorado Mountain College. She became professor emeritus at CMC. She is listed in the "Who's Who in American Women." She married Norvel Daniel. At age seventy she traveled around the country as a teacher of the Progoff Intensive Journal workshops. She died March 23, 2000, at the age of eighty-nine.

Margaret Durrance was born in San Francisco in 1917 and attended private schools in Pasadena and Berkeley studying art and music at the University of California. In 1937 she raced with the California Ski Team at Sun Valley and was invited to spend the rest of the winter training with the Ladies Olympic ski team. There she met Dick Durrance, Dartmouth's famous skier who was also training for the Olympics of 1940. They were married that summer and started Alta as a ski resort. In 1947, they moved to Aspen with their two small sons where Dick became the general manager of the new resort just beginning there. After five years, they went to Europe to make films, and it was then that she took up photography seriously. The years following were filled with traveling the world, photographing and filming Europe, Asia, the Middle East, China and South America. Her photographs have appeared in *Time, Life, Sports Illustrated, National Geographic, Venture, Snow Country,* and *Travel Holiday,* to name a few. She has recently become an associate of Photographers/Aspen.

Lee Ann King Eustis was born in 1935 in Philadelphia, Pennsylvania. She graduated from Vassar College in 1957. She worked at the N.W. Ayer Advertising Agency and *Kiplinger's Changing Times* magazine. She was married to George Pomeroy Eustis in 1962. She has two children, a daughter, Leslie Hallowell, and a son, Evan, who lives in Oakland. She has three Hallowell grandchildren. Since coming to Carbondale in 1965 to teach with her husband at CRMS, Lee Ann has centered her work and interest in education which includes serving as a board member for CRMS, for the Mt. Sopris Montessori School and the Carbondale Public Education Foundation. She has been a vigorous supporter of the arts.

Dorothea Farris was educated at New Jersey College for women and at the University of Colorado. She taught in Kirkland, Washington and in Carbondale, Basalt, and Aspen, Colorado. She and her husband, Doug Farris, lived in Woody Creek where they raised their children, Donald, Brian, and Anne. Her interest in public education, commitment to outdoor and experimental learning, and dedication to children led to a twenty-year career as a member of the Aspen

Board of Education and the Colorado Association of School Boards. Elected to the position in 1996, she currently works as a county commissioner in Pitkin County. Preservation of the natural world, protection of the special qualities of life where we find ourselves, recognition of the value of independent thinking and honest life choices, and a belief that the world should be one without borders direct the activities that give meaning to her life.

Annie Farris was raised in Woody Creek, educated in the Aspen Public schools and the University of Colorado. She has followed dual careers as a Montessori toddler teacher and a biological technician for the National Park Service. These interests have taken her to Hawaii, Alaska, Colorado, and the Pacific Northwest to study whales, spotted owls, raptors, peregrine falcons, amphibians, and young children.

Pat O'Neil Fender was born in Denver in 1928 and lived in Connecticut and Missouri. She attended the Perry Mansfield Camp in Steamboat Springs, Colorado starting in 1939. It is a wonderfully creative and beautiful spot with an emphasis on dance and drama. She avoided these as much as possible and spent her happiest hours at the stables. She graduated from Vassar College in 1950. Her first job, beyond being a camp counselor, was as a first grade teacher in a little copper-mining town in southeast Arizona. As a teacher of English in Carbondale, Colorado, she met Bill Fender on the way to a 4-H auction in Rifle in September of 1951. "He was a genuine Carbondale native." They were married in July of 1954 and she started working part-time for Colorado Rocky Mountain School the following September. She finished thirty-nine years of work there in 1996. They have two children. They are still living on their ranch in Emma, now run by their son.

Mary Lamprecht Ferguson was born May 5, 1906, in Spring Gulch, which was then a thriving coal mining town west of Carbondale. She lived in Carbondale her entire life. A teacher for thirty-seven years, Mary taught at the one-room schoolhouse on Missouri Heights near the Strang Ranch. She taught home economics at Carbondale Union High School and elementary school as well. She was recognized for her community service with many awards, including Carbondale Woman of the Year and most recently Volunteer of the Year from the Retired Seniors Volunteer Program. She served on the Carbondale town council. She also received the highest decoration bestowed on Rebekah, the Decoration of Chivalry, and she was honored as the grand marshal of the Potato Day Parade. She and her husband, Jack Ferguson, had four sons. Mary died in March of 1999. She was ninety-two.

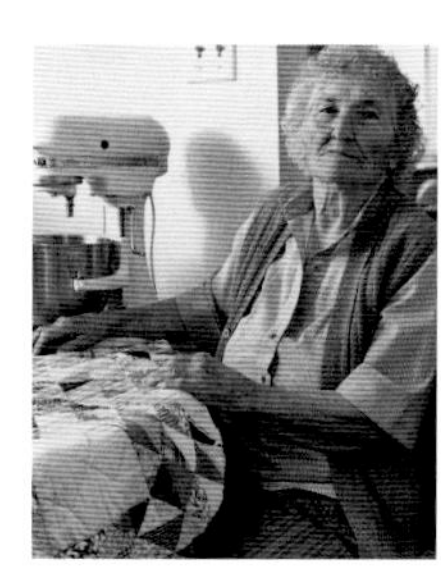

Marlyn McCrady Fiscus was born May 5, 1912, in Hughston, California, to Fred and Edna McCrady. She grew up in New Raymer, Colorado and graduated from high school there. She married Lyal Fiscus in 1933. He died January 21, 1981. Marlyn lived in Carbondale for fifty-six years and was a lunch cook at the Colorado Rocky Mountain School for forty years. She was a member of the Methodist Church and the Rebekahs and attained the rank of the Noble Grand. Marlyn and Lyal had one son and three daughters, fifteen grandchildren, thirty great-grandchildren and two great-great-grandchildren. Maryln died August 20, 2000 in Carbondale. She was eighty-seven.

Violet (Patsy) Sweetser Forbes was born April 13, 1924 in Brookline, Massachusetts. She was raised in New York city where her father was head of Bigelow Sanford Carpet Company. She was schooled in all girls private schools which she considers unfortunate. She never shared foibles and skin problems with boys and blames her innocence and abundance of marriages on that. She has four children, eleven grandchildren and one, very new great-granddaughter. She has been a teacher and writer, and now has settled down to paint portraits of her children. She lives in Boulder, Colorado after living in Aspen from 1958 to 1975. She thanks husband Gordon Forbes for removing her from Republican land in the East.

Janice Kirkpatrick Forbes was born October 13, 1952 in Austin, Minnesota. When she entered George School, a coed, Quaker boarding school, her tomboy nature thrived. Janice graduated from Ithaca College, where she made the U.S. Women's Field Hockey team. She has been an English teacher, coach of field hockey, soccer and lacrosse, and after being trained in the Montessori method, taught preschool and kindergarten, started her own Montessori kindergarten and traveled to Thailand to introduce Montessori materials to children and adults in a refugee camp. In 1986 she and her husband Arthur O. Forbes came to Carbondale where he accepted a job at CRMS. She now teaches at the extended day Montessori kindergarten at the Crystal River Elementary School. She and AO have three children.

Kate Kirkpatrick Forbes was born May 11, 1982 and from the age of four lived in Carbondale, Colorado. She attended the Mt. Sopris Montessori School, the Aspen Community School which her grandmother, Patsy, helped start and Colorado Rocky Mountain School. She is now a freshman at the University of Colorado.

Dottie Fox is a native Coloradan and has lived in the Roaring Fork Valley for over thirty years. She has four children, three of whom live nearby and one in Crestone, Colorado. Her service has included being Chairwoman of the Aspen Wilderness Workshop for the past fifteen years, Founder and board member of the Great Old Broads for Wilderness, twelve years on the board of Aspen Center for Environmental Studies, ten years on the board of the Southern Utah Wilderness Alliance, nine years on the Pitkin County Board of Adjustment, President of the League of Women Voters of Aspen and President of the Roaring Fork group of the Sierra Club. She has also been a watercolor art teacher for CMC.

Margaret Gallegos was born in 1923 in Taos, New Mexico and has lived in Carbondale for six years. She lives and is very active in the Senior Housing Community and in St. Marys of the Crown Church. She has two children, six grandchildren, and thirteen great-grandchildren.

Mary Glassier was born Mary Diemoz in 1912 in Marble. Her family moved from Marble when she was three months old and ran a ranch along the Catherine Store Road. She married Louis Glassier, also a child of immigrants from northern Italy. They lived for a while on the Glassier ranch, bought and ran the Catherine Store for four years, then bought the blacksmith shop which is now the village Smithy Restaurant. Later they ran a sawmill in Marble where they also ranched. She lived in Carbondale until 2000.

Adele MacDonald Hause was born in Denver in 1936. Her love for the mountains began in the Junior Colorado Mountain Club. She graduated from the University of Northern Colorado in 1958 and did graduate work at Colorado State University. She accompanied her husband Ken to teach at the Colorado Rocky Mountain School. There, they raised their four children, Heather, Kea, Eric, and Ian. Heather and Kea remain in the Roaring Fork Valley. In addition to the wonderful experiences with these children, Adele enjoyed teaching at the CRMS, directing a preschool and finally becoming the Alumni Director of the school in 1979, a calling which she has continued until 2001. She lives with her husband, Lester Bickel, in Carbondale.

Connie Harvey was born in Vienna, Austria, the only child of a divorced American mother, who was there to study medicine. With the advent of the Hitler years, Connie's mother joined the anti-Nazi underground, and helped many people to escape, including an Austrian whom she later married. After interludes in Paris and New York City, the family moved to a New Jersey farm. She went to McGill University in Montreal, and was on the ski team. After graduation, she went to Sun Valley and became a ski bum and part-time substitute teacher. In 1955, she married Dr. Harold Harvey and moved back to New Jersey. Three children later, on a ski trip to Aspen, they bought a home along Maroon Creek that the family still owns, and moved there in 1959. Connie taught skiing at Aspen Highlands, had three more children, and became an advocate for wilderness after passage of the Wilderness Act of 1964. In 1962, the Harveys bought a cattle ranch above Snowmass Creek. The children are grown now, and most have left the valley. Harold Harvey died in 1992. Connie remains active in ranching, writes a weekly column for the *Aspen Daily News*, and continues to work with the Aspen Wilderness Workshop which she founded with her friend and neighbor, Joy Caudill.

Mary Eshbaugh Hayes was born September 27, 1928 in Rochester, New York and grew up in New York state. She earned degrees in journalism and English at Syracuse University in 1950. She has worked on newspapers part-time since the age of fourteen. She came to Aspen in 1952 and has worked for *The Aspen Times* the last forty-three years, fifteen years as managing editor. She is the winner of many state and national awards for her writing and photography. She was named Colorado Press Woman of Achievement in 1986. She wrote *Aspen Potpourri*, a cookbook featuring the photographs of Aspenites along with their recipes and *The Story of Aspen*, a collection of newspaper and magazine articles and photographs covering stories from 1881 to the present. She married silversmith Jim Hayes and is the mother five children.

Bates Hayes was born in Aspen in 1962, lived there for twenty-five years and in Basalt for fifteen years. A master silver and goldsmith and award-winning oil painter, Bates and her husband spent many years making the famous Aspen Leaf jewelry designed by her father, Jim Hayes. She painted the daily lives of many local Basalt townsfolk and showed her work at a national level. She works to improve the community by organizing mural projects, building parks, and serving on various planning committees.

Jane Jochems Hendricks was born July 26, 1941 in Wichita, Kansas. She still loves the plains. She graduated from Stanford University in 1963 and moved to Satank, Colorado in 1966 to teach at the Colorado Rocky Mountain School. She and her husband Brad built a log cabin in 1972 which they expanded. Surrounding the log home are gardens. For some time Jane was part owner of the *Roaring Fork Valley Journal*. She and Brad had three children, Harmony, Hillary, and Heidi. Harmony and her husband have a baby girl named Moxie Wyoming (the family has attachments to Wyoming). Harmony and Heidi are helping build a home out of logs now near Collbran, Colorado. They have peeled, planed and notched the logs. Hillary helps Jane with her newest venture, The Rocky Mountain Flamingo in Collbran, specializing in home-cooked, red-neck food.

Eve Homeyer was born in 1915 in North Platte, Nebraska. She and her husband had visited Aspen and when he died in the early sixties, she decided she would try living there. She opened a shop, the House of Ireland, until Irish linen became very expensive. She was mayor of Aspen from 1970 until 1973. It was during that time due to a remark she made casually about driving that she decided she would no longer depend on a car. She has not driven since and she attributes her good health to the fact that she walks and uses public transportation. Currently she works for a group she started, Senior Independent, which raises money for activities for seniors, not bricks and mortar.

Rebecca Hutton was born in 1912 in Taos, New Mexico and came with her husband, Bob, and their four children to Carbondale in 1969. For eighteen years she worked as a cook at Colorado Rocky Mountain School. She has been housekeeper and cook for many families in the Roaring Fork Valley for the last thirty years. She has six grandchildren and three great-grandchildren.

Louise van K. Jackson was born in Philadelphia, Pennsylvania in 1925. She received her degree in chemistry from Mount Holyoke College and married Carter Jackson in 1948. She and her veterinarian husband have lived for the past forty-nine years on their ranch south of Glenwood Springs. They have raised four daughters and are also proud of their seven granddaughters. Louise has been a very active community member. Chipeta Girl Scout Council recently named their new outdoor center in her honor.

Virginia Lappala was born Virginia Denmead on March 24, 1917 near West Liberty, Ohio. She attended Antioch College where she met her husband, Paul. They came to Carbondale in 1971. They bought the building, now the site of the Village Smithy, intending to turn it into dormitory space for CMC students though it became first a preschool, a weaving center, fish store and finally the Smithy. They also restored the building which is now 6/89, lived in it and eventually bought the entire block it is on enabling them later to give nine of the lots to CMC where the college built the Lappala Center. Gini has been "involved with the Quakers from the word go." The Lappalas lived in Hong Kong where they worked on a social service project through the American Friends Service Committee. They also helped with a project making limbs for the Vietnamese. Gini was named Carbondale Woman of the Year in 1998 for her service in Carbondale. Her passion has been helping children and adults learn to read. She has tutored dyslexic children and adults, helped with senior citizens and been a member of several organizations.

Isabel Pfrimmer Hays Mace was born on September 13, 1918 in Corydon, Indiana. She attended Grinnell College where she met Stuart Aitken Mace. They were married in 1947 and in 1949, the Maces opened Toklat Wilderness Lodge at Ashcroft, their home and place of business. Here they raised five children while participating in innumerable community affairs and running many different businesses: lodge, restaurant, husky kennel, and handcrafted art gallery. Isabel lives part-time at Toklat with her daughter, who now manages the business, and part-time with her three sons in southern Colorado. Stuart died in August, 1993 and their eldest son, Greg, died in a mountain climbing accident in July, 1986.

Lynne Pfrimmer Mace was born September 28, 1945. She grew up in Aspen, attending all twelve grades at the Red Brick School House. She graduated from George Washington University in 1970. She married in March, 1970 and moved to England with her husband. Returning to the U.S. in 1974, they settled in Sharon, Connecticut where Lynne was active in many community affairs. In 1986, they moved to Paris, France where they lived until 1991. Divorced in 1995, Lynne returned to Toklat and has managed the business for her mother since 1996.

Pat Maddalone was born in Aspen in 1928. Her parents were Maymie Crosby Kearns and Owen Kearns. She was a wife and later a widow of Edward Popish and a mother of Marlene Popish Maddelone and a widow of Charles Maddelone. She was an accountant in the Aspen Valley Hospital. For about 30 years Pat worked as business manager for both firms, Benedict Associates and Benedict Land and Cattle Company. She also served on several community boards including the Aspen School Board and the Aspen Hospital Board.

Marie Baumgartner-Maurin was born in Neudorf, Lucerne Switzerland. She was the only woman in the Baumgartner family to leave Switzerland. Marie's mother passed away just before she turned sixteen and she eventually persuaded her father to let her stay home from school to take care of the family which she did until she was twenty-one. She traveled and worked in Paris and England. There she met and married and American GI, George Maurin. She took her place as a Colorado ranch wife on Capitol Creek and raised their two children, Dwight and Judy. She was able to return to Switzerland in 1985 to visit her last remaining brother. She is proud of her four grandchildren and now is happily living with her daughter, Judy, and husband, Bill, in Lawton, Oklahoma.

Laurie Mack McBride was born in Pasadena, California in 1939. She attended Stanford University and spent her junior year at the Sorbonne in Paris. She was married in 1964 to John McBride and moved to Vail, Colorado. In 1966 they moved to Aspen and in 1980 moved to Old Snowmass where they now live on the Lost Marbles Ranch. They have three children, John Jr. who is a coach for the U.S. Men's alpine ski team, Kate McBride, and Peter McBride, photojournalist. Laurie is a designer, watercolorist, gardener, skier, tennis player, hiker, loves living on a ranch, and works hard to save animals. She serves on the Wildlife Trust board founded by Gerald Durrell.

Kate McBride was born in Pasadena, California, raised in Aspen and graduated from Princeton University. She has her commercial multi-engine instrument rated pilot's license and says her "true loves of life are acrobatic flying and air combat." She was on the World Pro Ski Tour from 1994-98 and is a six-time and current world record holder of 24 Hours of Aspen. She married Casey Puckett in July of 2000.

Paula Mechau, née Paula Ralska, was born in 1907 and grew up on Long Island. An aspiring actress, she left home after high school to go on tour. She returned to New York and married Colorado artist Frank Mechau. Shortly thereafter, the couple went to Europe, residing in Paris where Frank was able to study and paint, Paula doing advertising for Dorothy Gray Cosmetics. After three years, they returned to the U.S., and in 1937 settled in Redstone, then a ghost town. In 1946 Paula's beloved husband suddenly died, leaving her with four young children: Vanni, Dorik, Duna, and Mike. In these difficult circumstances, she and the children helped sustain themselves folksinging, and Paula worked at various jobs: in Colorado Springs, as secretary to the American composer Roy Harris; in Grand Junction, teaching folksinging in the public schools; finally, happily returning home to Redstone to work in Carbondale as secretary to John and Anne Holden, the founders of the Colorado Rocky Mountain School. She continued to work in many capacities including teacher (of literature and weaving) and librarian for the rest of her career. Today in her ninety-fourth year, she still serves as an honorary board member of Colorado Rocky Mountain School.

Dolores Montoya was born in 1948 in Taos, New Mexico and has lived in Carbondale with her husband Andy, daughter Andrea, and son, John for ten years. Dolores taught ESL to adults for Colorado Mountain College and now teaches ESL to first and second graders. Her husband, Andy, is on the Carbondale Town Council and they are both active in Carbondale politics and the life of their grandson, Levi.

Emmy Neil was born in Denver in 1923. In 1935 the family moved to Burns, Colorado. Emmy attended high school in Denver and graduated from Denver University. She met her husband, Cliff, in Burns and they moved to Glenwood Springs in 1953. Over the years she has been a leader of Girl Scouts, Cub Scouts and 4-H. She was one of the first instructors at Colorado Mountain College where she continues to teach needle arts, classes where students also learn more about being better individuals and community members. She is a member of the Glenwood Springs sister city board of directors and takes regular trips to Teote where she began a sewing cooperative for local women. She has been named Colorado's Business and Professional Woman of the Year and Colorado Citizen of the Year. A room named the "Emmy Neil" room can be found in the Glenwood center of CMC.

Ruth (Ditty) Perry is the daughter of Aspen pioneer DRC Brown who lived from 1880-1930. She attended Kent School in Denver and Mills College. She married Robert (Bob) Perry in 1940 and has been ranching in Carbondale for sixty years, raising Hereford cattle and quarter horses. The Perrys have seven children: Robin, Rosamond, Ruthie, Nancy, Will, Marjorie, and Charlotte.

Betty Pfister was born in Great Neck, New York in 1921. She graduated from Bennington College in Bennington, Vermont in 1943. She flew for two years during WWII as a member of the WASPs, ferrying many types of military aircraft all over the U.S. In 1954 she married Art Pfister and they moved to Aspen, Colorado. They have three grown daughters and five grandchildren. Her interest and involvement in flying has remained constant over all these years. It has been a source of great pleasure during her entire life.

Winifred Conway Rector was born September 4, 1916 in Walsenburg, Colorado. She lived in Durango, Rangley, and finally came to Carbondale in 1960. She concentrated all of her life on her family, friends and church. She was a member of St. Mary's of the Crown in Carbondale. She and her husband, Bill, had four children, three daughters and a son, now deceased. One of her loves was an informal community prayer group. She had five great-grandchildren when she died June 8, 1998.

Peggy Cooper Rowland was born in 1915 in Aspen. Her mother, Fleeta Lamb Cooper, was born in 1888 in Aspen. Her grandfather, Al S. Lamb, came to Aspen in 1881 and her father, Edward Cooper, had a bookstore on Galena Street. Peggy graduated from Colorado State University in Home Economics and taught in Loveland, Colorado before marrying Harold (Red) Rowland. Red was also born in Aspen in 1908 and died in 1987. Peggy taught in Aspen, was past state president of P.E.O., volunteered at The Thrift Shop and the Historical Society, and was inducted into the Aspen Hall of Fame. She belongs to Christ Episcopal Church. Peggy and Red had four children: Fleeta Rowland Baldwin, Roine Rowland St. Andrew, Jack Rowland and twin sister Jill Rowland Boyd. They also have three grandchildren and three great-grandchildren. Peggy lives on Shady Lane in Aspen.

Roine Rowland St. Andre was born in Denver in 1942 because her parents had moved from Aspen due to lack of work. In 1946 the family returned to Aspen. She attended all twelve grades at The Red Brick School and was on the ski team during her high school years. She graduated in 1960 and attended CSU and then Western State College in Gunnison where she met her husband. In 1969 she was the first woman ski patroller the Aspen Ski Corp. hired. She had that job for twenty-nine years. She and her husband, Jon, finally built their home on Spring Creek. Their house is build of recycled materials, uses solar power, and water is pumped with an old-fashioned hydro ram.

Alice Rachel Peck Sardy was born September 6, 1908 in Circleville, Ohio. The family moved to the San Luis Valley in 1910. Alice Rachel attended Western State College in Gunnison and received and A.B. in Business and Education in 1932. She married Tom Sardy in 1936. Tom bought the hardware store and mortuary when they moved to Aspen. Tom and Alice Rachel had a daughter, Sylvia and son, Thomas Jay. Sylvia and her husband live in Tuscaloosa, Alabama and T.J. resides in Anchorage, Alaska. Alice Rachel was one of the first original volunteers for the hospital. She also was a volunteer for the Aspen Historical Society and the Aspen Chapel.

Betsy Schenck was born May 12, 1927 in Denver Colorado. She received a B.S. in music from Colorado College and an M.S. in music from C.U. Boulder. She married Robert Schenck in 1951. They moved to Carbondale in 1960. She began teaching at CMC, gradually becoming a full-time professor of music and drama, all the while rearing six children through the Carbondale Public School system. Her children are Susan, Barbara, Robert, Jr., Patricia, Paula, and John. The Schencks have eleven grandchildren. At present she is the organist/pianist at St. Barnabas Episcopal Church in Glenwood Springs.

Suzi Sewell was born in Denver August 7, 1947. She moved to the Roaring Fork Valley with her parents in 1951 and attended school in Basalt. Her husband, Bob Sewell, and sons, Jason and Alex, were born and grew up on their ranch in south Carbondale.

Barbara Morris Snobble grew up in Highland Park, Illinois. She graduated from Vassar College in 1946 and was married (eloped) in Aspen in 1947. She lived in Colorado Springs, France, Austria, Germany, and Washington, D.C. before moving to Carbondale in 1954 to help start the Colorado Rocky Mountain School. She taught there until 1969. She continued teaching at CMC soon after it opened. She helped found and was officer of the Crystal Valley Environmental Protections Association, the Mt. Sopris Historical Society and the Carbondale Council on Arts and Humanities. She was the director for the Gordon Cooper Library and a member of the Carbondale Parks and Recreation Board. She and her husband Jack had four daughters: Cori, Cassi, Conne, and Chrisie.

Louiva P. Stapleton was born October 28, 1913, in Collbran, Colorado and moved to Aspen at the age of seven. She was raised by her great-aunt, Ella Stallard, in the Stallard home which is now the Stallard House Museum. She married William C. Stapleton in 1933 and they had four children, twelve grandchildren and eleven great-grandchildren. Louiva was one of the original founders of The Thrift Shop in Aspen and volunteered in the gift shop at Aspen Valley Hospital for twenty-one years. She shared the Greg Mace Award for volunteerism in the Aspen area. Louiva lived in Aspen's West End for sixty-two years. She died March 15, 2000. She was eighty-six years old.

Kit Strang was born in Milwaukee, Wisconsin February 1, 1934. She graduated from Vassar College with a BS in geology in 1956. She was employed in the oil industry and ski industry. In 1960 she married Michael Strang. The Strangs have four children: Lathrop, Laurie, Scott and Bridget and three grandchildren. They have lived on the Strang Ranch above Carbondale since 1965. They raise cattle, horses, a few sheep and hay. They also have a turf farm and an active horse business in which they teach, train, and show. Kit has been involved in all of it in various ways and especially during her husband's political adventures as a representative to the U.S. Congress. She is active in a variety of community activities including the Pony Club and Western Colorado Heritage Fund.

Bleu Stroud was born August 6 "a long time ago," in western Nebraska and moved to California immediately after she graduated from high school. She and her husband moved to Marble, Colorado in 1957 and started building their house which "they never really finished." She is a charter member of the Glenwood Springs Art Guild, a member of the Redstone Art Association, the Marble Art Association and the Marble Historical Society. In 1959, with a few good friends, she began helping renovate the long-vacant, abandoned little church in Marble. Choir rails were dug from backyard trash and broken windows and unhinged doors fixed. It now has year-round services.

Amelia Cullet Trentaz was born February 15, 1919 in Aspen, Colorado. She lived for seven years in Aspen, then moved to a small ranch in Canyon Creek eight miles west of Glenwood Springs, where she graduated from high school. She attended Mesa College and Colorado University. She married Arthur Trentaz in 1940. Their ranch was sold in 1962 and they moved into Aspen where she worked as a library assistant until 1979. She volunteered at The Thrift Shop for thirty years, the Aspen Historical Museum for twenty-five years, and the library. She returned to Glenwood Springs in 1994 and currently volunteers at the senior center and Valley View Hospital. They have two children, Fred and Mary Lou.

Rosamond Perry Turnbull was raised on the Perry Ranch and attended school in Carbondale. She graduated from CRMS and Colorado College. She and her husband Tom live on the Four-Bar Ranch and have two sons and two daughters. She has been a member of the Agriculture and Cultural Leadership Group and Chairman of the Pitkin County Agriculture Planning Board.

Gretl Uhl was born on November 3, 1923 in Bad Toelz, Germany and raised in Germisch-Partenkrichen, Germany. Her parents owned a restaurant in the Olympic Skistadium in Partenkirchen. She raced on the German national alpine team from 1941-1951. In 1948 Gretl and her husband, Sepp, were married and shortly after, in 1953 they immigrated to Aspen. In 1957, Gretl became a certified instructor on Aspen Mountain and was the first female instructor to have accelerated classes. From 1959-1962 she was one of the directors for Southern Rocky Mountain Ski Instructors Association. She opened "Gretl's" restaurant in Tourtelotte Park on Aspen Mountain in 1966 and ran it until 1980. For five years beginning in 1982 Gretl worked as a consultant for Aspen Highlands Merry Go Round restaurant. She has two children. Today she is retired and loves to travel, loves her friends and loves Aspen.

Martha Downer Waterman now lives in Basalt. She operates a B&B in her home on seven acres of the 180-acre ranch that she and Leroy Waterman bought in 1960. Her son and his wife have a home on the property. In 1996 Martha sold the rest of the property to the Roaring Fork Club for a golf course. Martha has a daughter living in Glenwood Springs and a grandson in Steamboat Springs. She enjoys spending time with her grandchildren and playing bridge.

Mary Downer Evans moved from Colorado in 1993 to Walla Walla, Washington to be closer to her daughter. She was diagnosed with Parkinson's disease in 1992, and while it slowed her down a bit, she still has a lot of spunk. At eighty-five, Mary still has a wonderful sense of humor and sparkle in her eyes.

Polly Whitcomb was born in Connecticut in 1931 and grew up in Illinois. She and her first husband, Buzz Bent, with a friend Joey Cabell, opened the Chart House in 1963. After they were divorced, she moved to Boulder with her daughters, Verena and Thea, to complete her BA in English and education. She married Dr. Harald Whitcomb in 1968 and, with his children, Michael and Dierdre, created their family. Their son Oliver was born in 1970, the same year they joined with several other families to found the Aspen Community School, an alternative K-8 school in Woody Creek. For the past thirty years, she has been involved with the school as a board member, poetry teacher, and lyricist for the annual school musical.

Luetta Whitson was born September 15, 1931 in Aspen to Maymie Crosby Kearns and Owen Kearns. She attended elementary school at The Little Red Schoolhouse and graduated from Aspen High School in 1948. She worked in Aspen at the Golden Horn from 1954-7 and at the Hotel Jerome until 1964. She worked for the Aspen Ski Corporation as payroll clerk, as assistant controller and eventually as controller until 1992. She continued working part-time in accounting through 1997. In addition to her sister Pat Maddelone, her family consists of a daughter and son-in-law, two granddaughters and four great-grandsons.

Anita Witt was born in Wichita, Kansas September 13, 1938. As a youngster, she was an entertainer and performed with a group of young musicians on a Wichita TV station for many years. She was a trick rider and did shows in rodeos in Kansas and Oklahoma. She graduated from Oklahoma State University in 1961 and taught school for a short time before becoming an entertainer again, working in many places including Las Vegas, Chicago and New York. In 1966, she married Don Witt, and they moved to the ranch on Missouri Heights which Anita still owns today. They built and operated Center Drug for twenty-three years. When her husband Don passed away in 1993, Anita went back to work as an entertainer, singing and playing guitar in many fine area restaurants. She also does a rodeo act of trick roping with her dog Sadie and beautiful trick horse Whiskey.

Ruth Whyte was born in Kenosha, Wisconsin in 1928. She graduated from the University of Colorado with a B.S. in physical education in 1951 and moved to Aspen in 1952 where she was involved with the Aspen Ski Club, The Winterskol Committee, the Roch Cup, and the Aspen Historical Society to name a few. She received the Greg Mace Award in 1992 for Outstanding Volunteerism and in 1996 was inducted into the Aspen Hall of Fame.

Beulah Wilson came with her husband Bailey Sterrett to the Roaring Fork Valley in 1929. Bailey Sterrett died in 1945 and Beulah married John Wilson. John and Bailey were ranchers and second cousins. Beulah was instrumental in establishing the Carbondale Fire District, the Gordon Cooper Library, the Rebekah's New Year Store, the Tri-County Medical Clinic and Carbondale Senior Housing. She was a member of the Rebekah Lodge, Eastern Star and the Methodist Church Ladies Aid. She was also a social services case worker for Garfield County for 24 years, retiring in 1957 as the county's director of public welfare. Beulah had two daughters, one son, nine grandchildren, thirty-eight great- and great-great-grandchildren. Beulah died June 21, 1999, at her home outside Carbondale. She was ninety-nine years old.